'Being able to transform an organisation is the 'must-have' skill for the 21st century. Michael and Graham combine the proven techniques of top executives and consultants with real world insights and experience to offer a complete insiders field guide. This book is a must for anyone involved in leading change that will enrich their understanding of what it really takes to transform a company, division, function or team.'
—Olaf Pietschner, CEO Capgemini Asia Pacific & Middle East

'The message is clear, transform or watch your company and its fortunes diminish or disappear. Vullings and Christie apply their wealth of lived industry experience to bring a must-read, practical guide for leaders to create change and build the capabilities they need to transform their organisation and build sustainable competitive advantage. *Changing the Game* is not just theory, rather a step by step guide to transformation.'
—Mark Buckman, Former Chief Marketing Officer, Commonwealth Bank of Australia; Former Chief Marketing Officer, Telstra; Past Forbes World's Most Influential CMOs List.

'Digital technology is transforming organisations at an unprecedented pace. *Changing the Game* offers the blueprint for staying ahead of the curve. Enabling organisations to thrive rather than survive, this enlightening book offers a practical framework that you can use to drive and shape the future of your business. A must read for any executive navigating change in their organisation.'
—Tamara Oppen, Managing Director, GoDaddy Australia

T0359465

CHANGING
THE GAME

CHANGING
THE GAME

THE PLAYBOOK FOR
LEADING BUSINESS
TRANSFORMATION

MICHAEL VULLINGS
GRAHAM CHRISTIE

WILEY

First published in 2021 by John Wiley & Sons Australia, Ltd
42 McDougall St, Milton Qld 4064

Office also in Melbourne

Typeset in Utopia Std 10.5/15pt

ISBN: 978-0-730-38913-2

A catalogue record for this
book is available from the
National Library of Australia

NATIONAL
LIBRARY
OF AUSTRALIA

Cover design by Wiley

Disclaimer
The material in this publication is of the nature of general comment only, and does not represent professional advice. It is not intended to provide specific guidance for particular circumstances and it should not be relied on as the basis for any decision to take action or not take action on any matter which it covers. Readers should obtain professional advice where appropriate, before making any such decision. To the maximum extent permitted by law, the authors and publisher disclaim all responsibility and liability to any person, arising directly or indirectly from any person taking or not taking action based on the information in this publication.

Printed in Singapore
M113277_040521

CONTENTS

FOREWORD

Digital technology is changing the way we live and the way we work, and is a key driver of transformational change across all industries.

The opportunities for businesses are tremendous, and are arriving faster than anticipated due to accelerated digital transformation spurred by the COVID-19 pandemic.

Leading companies through major change is not for the faint-hearted; it takes strong vision, empathy, drive and, above all, a robust but flexible plan.

Organisations need talented leaders to navigate this change and forge a new path — individuals who possess the ability to drive a dramatic step-change in company performance with confidence and skills to negotiate ever-changing, dynamic markets.

With 35 years of industry knowledge behind them, Michael and Graham are no strangers to digital innovation, and this book draws on their collective experience at the helm of organisations both large and small, steering them through major disruption and change.

The practical skills and know-how for leading business transformation are not things easily studied in a classroom, but rather draw on years of experience and hard-earned lessons. This is exactly what Michael and Graham bring to this book.

They have taken the essential elements required to transform companies, and — using approaches I frequently see among top executives and top management consulting firms — have distilled them into this practical and instructional playbook.

Top teams, executives and managers everywhere, regardless of their industry or expertise, will benefit from drawing on the practical tools, templates and approaches they outline.

In my roles as CEO of Telstra and IBM in Australia and New Zealand, I have had the privilege of overseeing the growth and development of the next generation of leaders in these companies and shaping them for tomorrow — not only as market leaders in their time, but to thrive in the decades ahead.

During my time at Telstra, the business underwent an incredible journey of change, pivoting towards the benefits of digitisation and utilising data, and setting up the Telstra Digital unit, which laid the foundations for Telstra's future, and remains at the core of how the business operates today.

Transformation requires not only top executives, but leaders at all levels of an organisation with the skills and fortitude to push the boundaries and find new and better ways to operate. This, together with the constant desire to reinvent the business, has been a vital ingredient of Telstra's success.

More recently I have had the honour of chairing the Board of CSIRO, Australia's national science agency. In my time as Chair, I have watched CSIRO transform not only its operations but the way it does research, bringing cutting edge technology to augment and enhance work in all science domains.

It has led to an acceleration in research to solve Australia's greatest challenges, demonstrating the tremendous value of digital technologies like artificial intelligence and machine learning to Australian innovation.

At such a pivotal time, when digital transformation is disrupting every industry and sector, it is valuable to have a manual and blueprint for adapting to this change.

Changing the Game is a practical guide to transforming companies, divisions and teams. Whether they are new to planning and implementing change or a seasoned veteran, this book will provide leaders with a framework, practical tools and a roadmap, so that they too can drive a step-change in their organisation, from start to finish.

David Thodey
December 2020

David Thodey AO has been at the forefront of Australian business for over three decades as a distinguished CEO and Chairperson. He has led some of Australia's most iconic organisations through periods of tremendous growth, transformation and shareholder value creation. In 2017, David was awarded the Order of Australia for his services to business and ethical leadership. He is widely recognised as one of the nation's top business leaders.

ACKNOWLEDGEMENTS

This book reflects the collective efforts of many people — so it is with a great deal of appreciation and gratitude that we thank our friends, families, colleagues and clients.

We would like to acknowledge the many friends and colleagues in our network who have given their time to review and provide feedback on drafts at various stages during the book's development, including Robert Kinkade, Sir Tim McClement KCB OBE, Michael Welch, Dr Marco Berti and Dr Dean Blomson. Their advice and feedback have been instrumental in shaping how we've described and presented the ideas and approaches we use in successfully working with executive teams, senior leaders and managers, and have helped us translate those ideas into a thoughtful and practical playbook. In particular, a special thank you to Jim Patrick AO, who has been a great source of feedback and encouragement during the process.

While writing this book, we've had numerous conversations with exceptional executives in many industries, who have shared their stories from leading transformations in some of the most iconic Australian and international organisations. We are grateful for their time and input into this book, which has helped to enhance and reinforce many important topics throughout.

In particular, for their support, time and valuable contributions, we would like to recognise the following executives (in alphabetical order):

Sir Tim McClement KCB OBE
Former Vice Admiral
British Royal Navy

Neil Robinson
Managing Director, Digital
News Corp Australia

Jim Patrick AO
Chief Scientist Emeritus
Cochlear Limited

Adam Warden
Former Senior Partner
Bain & Company

Michael Pratt AM
Secretary, NSW Treasury
NSW Government

Michael Welch
Former GM Transformation
National Broadband Network

PREFACE

Digital technologies are set to disrupt almost every industry sector, which means every company is facing a transformation agenda that can no longer be ignored. The concept of *digital transformation* has gained considerable attention in the media and corporate culture over the past decade, but the term is often misunderstood. Digital transformation as we define it in this book is not about substituting legacy systems with digital technologies. It is about *transforming* a company holistically, creating a step-change in organisational efficiency and customer intimacy supported by digital technology.

Customer expectations have increased dramatically as leading global companies transform entire industry sectors by reshaping and retooling their organisation, exploring new possibilities and adopting new ways of working. These new paradigms in turn now demand that companies constantly adapt and transform their businesses to stay relevant to their customers, competitive in their marketplace, and able to survive and thrive in the digital age.

Drawing on leading practices, *Changing the Game* is a playbook that looks well beyond specific technologies and digital trends. It equips the executive, irrespective of sector, with a strategic, actionable framework for transformational change. Used as a practical roadmap that considers important internal and external aspects of leading change, *Changing the Game* offers a straightforward, holistic approach, enhanced by relevant concepts and illustrations, brought to life with insights and real-world examples shared by outstanding leaders.

INTRODUCTION

This book sets out how to create a step-change in company performance. It's about how to get started, where to focus your effort, and what to do at each stage of the journey — but most importantly it's about how to get results.

The reality is that very few companies are able to sustain exceptional performance for any extended period of time. Most products, companies and even entire industries follow patterns of rapid early growth, steady maturity and eventual decline. To remain successful, companies must be effective at managing renewal, or risk losing relevance and being overtaken by competitors — a situation that, left unmanaged, can lead to eventual company failure and collapse — as was the case with Blockbuster, Kodak and Nokia, to name a few. However, managing renewal is something companies are rarely good at.

Changing the Game is not only for troubled companies in search of renewal. It's for all companies that, at least periodically, need to fundamentally enhance their trajectory. Many of the world's most successful companies, such as Apple, Amazon, General Electric, Google and Microsoft, reinvent themselves time and again to sustain their success and retain market leadership. But transforming a company, or even small parts of one, can be an enormous undertaking. Frequently, it can involve redefining the core capabilities of the organisation. This can be a confronting task for both management and employees and is often met with resistance, fear and uncertainty. However, with the right level of focus and planning many common pitfalls can be avoided.

We draw on leading practice to offer practical advice on how to design, manage and deliver a successful company transformation, and provide a basis from which you might take action within your own company. But first, let's look at how to recognise a need for action.

Crisis as a catalyst for change

At the core of every transformation is a crisis. This can take many forms: Where concerns are about the future, the crisis may be strategic so that the focus is on shifting the business model and building capabilities to maintain a sustainable competitive advantage that will enable the company to compete over the long term. On the other hand, in more distressed management situations, such as a turnaround scenario, the crisis may be financial and asset-related, with concerns typically about cash management and financing debt obligations to ensure short-term survival.

Deciding whether to 'change the game' begins with an assessment of a company's situation to establish the need for action. Leaders in the company should ask what internal and external challenges and opportunities they currently face, how quickly the current situation will change and what the timeframe for action will be. Transforming the company can require an objective look at the company's current financial and operating performance in order to decide whether there is an emerging case for change to which the company must respond. At other times, leaders can be forced into action by outside events, such as a financial market collapse, a global pandemic or a major shift in public policy. In both cases the resulting situation means that companies usually face one of three broad imperatives, based on the types of challenges and opportunities that exist and the immediacy of the situation (see figure I.1):

1   *Manage cash and liquidity.* Protect company solvency and ensure financial obligations are met, often with specialised outside support.

2   *Realign for profitability.* Overcome a trend in average or below-expectations performance, such as failure to meet sales or profitability targets.

3   *Build on existing success.* Sustain success or realise even greater results by responding to marketplace changes, building capabilities and acting on new opportunities to sustain competitive advantage.

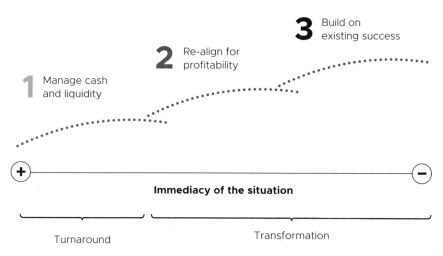

Figure I.1: recognising the need for action — three broad company imperatives

Companies building on existing success should be on the lookout for early signs of market transitions that lead to new opportunities. Leaders in these companies should ask what the trend breaks are and when the long-term situation is going to change. Early recognition of market shifts can provide significant opportunity to capitalise on these trends by proactively repositioning the company, making strategic bets and exploring sources of innovation to create viable future options.

For companies that operate in rapidly changing markets, transformation is no longer being seen as a 'one-off' event, as the market changes demand an 'always-on' transformation in which change and renewal are constant. This suggests that sources of both innovation and transformation are themselves becoming increasingly important capabilities that companies need to institutionalise or hardwire into how they operate. Creating an organisation that has the capacity to remake itself is not easy. At first a company may not have all the necessary capabilities, but over time it can establish processes and structures that build a culture in which adapting to change is part of the new normal.

A range of situations can signal that changing the game should be an essential part of a company's forward-management strategy. For a company that is performing strongly, this book provides a framework for sustaining success and delivering a step-change towards even greater results. If a company is facing uncertain market dynamics, increased competition and lacklustre financial results, *Changing the Game* offers a pathway to reinvention and growth. For companies already facing challenges, the mounting pressure for change will require an immediate coordinated and systematic response. In each of these situations, *Changing the Game* provides the framework, methods and tools to take action and drive results.

An integrated approach to transformation

While transformation programs need to be tailored to each company's unique situation and context, companies that are successful in transforming often deploy an orthodox set of tools and methods. While the imperatives for change and the scale of the effort required can vary widely from company to company, there are many common elements, including assessing existing performance; exploring key issues and opportunities; establishing a bold and ambitious vision for the future; developing a robust strategy; ensuring funding, skills and resources; and sustaining momentum over the course of a multi-year program. So it is not surprising that undertaking a major transformation — whether to identify and act on opportunities or to respond to a crisis — can successfully utilise many of the same tools and approaches to achieve excellent results in a wide range of cases.

This book will equip leaders and their companies to implement a major transformation through five stages that together represent a complete journey (see figure I.2). These five stages form a dynamic approach for planning, designing, managing and delivering a transformation program, and provide a systematic way to overcome many of the common barriers to change. Sometimes leaders choose to improvise and take short cuts, but a disciplined, methodical application of leading practices will dramatically improve the degree of success. *Changing the Game*'s strategies are applicable whether the focus of the transformation is enterprise-wide or confined to a single business unit, function or market, and whether a distressed company needs a rapid and effective turnaround or a good company aspires to become a great one.

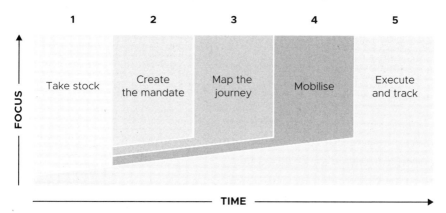

Figure I.2: stages in the transformation journey

A complete transformation journey can be divided into the following five key steps:

1   *Take stock*. Assess the company and its operating environment to identify and prioritise key opportunities, ensure operational and

financial stability, lay foundations by mobilising a top team who have bought into the idea, and build credibility through quick wins.

2   *Create the mandate.* Establish a common view of where the company is today, along with the opportunities and challenges faced, in order to build an objective 'base case' and a trajectory based on current performance.

3   *Map the journey.* Create a compelling vision for the future and develop high-level aspirations with clear targets that lead to a common direction and shared sense of purpose in order to explore strategic themes and initiatives. Then commit to a plan of action that will lead the company to the newly imagined future.

4   *Mobilise.* Create a strong foundation for delivery by preparing the company for change: clearly communicate the company strategy to employees and other stakeholders; remove obstacles and create incentives; keep promoting change; establish a transformation office (TO) to coordinate efforts.

5   *Execute and track.* Develop detailed solutions and assign ownership. Ensure resources are available and establish routines to drive and monitor progress (including a review cadence, performance monitoring, and root-cause troubleshooting) to sustain initiative delivery and enable the company to capture the full potential of the transformation.

Driving results at each step along the transformation journey requires leadership, time and persistence. Getting started often requires a considerable upfront investment in people, planning and quick action to secure visible short-term results that will boost momentum. With the right levels of sponsorship and a dedicated team in place, the overall process of planning the transformation can be accomplished relatively quickly. The mobilisation and execution of initiatives that follow the planning can then span months or years, depending on the scale, scope and nature of the changes the company must make to achieve its vision.

Each major step in a transformation and how long it is likely to take is outlined in figure I.3. The sequence, key deliverables and timeframes are

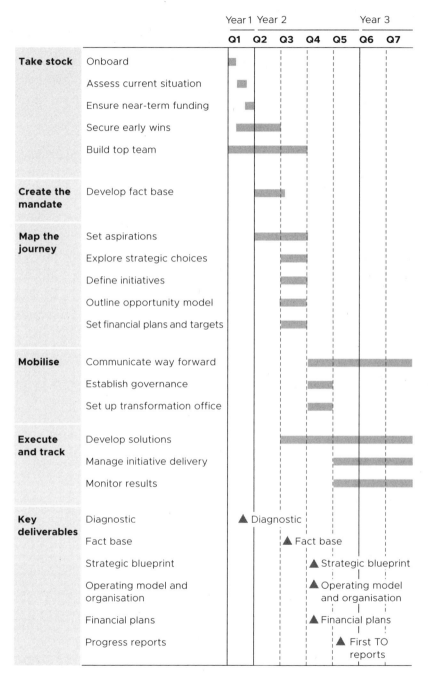

Figure I.3: illustrative transformation high-level phasing — key activities

illustrative and will vary. It takes longer to transform a company with, for example, vast and complex operations, more complicated organisational politics and longer operating cycles than to transform a smaller, agile company in a fast-paced industry. Whatever the timeframe is, adopting a phased approach and clear milestones not only makes the journey more manageable but provides a clear pathway to success.

The chapters in this book are organised according to the five stages outlined and cover the essential activities at each step. Each chapter provides not just explanations but practical examples that bring the journey to life. Examples are drawn from public sources and interviews with leading global executives. However, because many aspects of specific transformation programs are managed in strict confidence and inside company walls, the authors have supplemented examples with tailored content based on their knowledge and experience so as to provide a comprehensive guide for taking action in your own company.

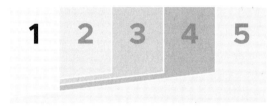

Take stock

A common first stage of a transformation is to assess the present condition of the company. The breadth and depth of a quick assessment will differ, but the objective remains the same: an *initial point-of-view* of the present strategic, operating and financial health of the company, including an overview of the challenges and opportunities, and drawing attention to any issues that require immediate attention.

A quick assessment or health check is typically initiated by top management or the Board to obtain an independent, objective, fact-based assessment of the situation. Use of external parties such as consultants or external advisers can assist in identifying issues, gathering data, conducting analysis, synthesising findings and providing recommendations. However, the assessment should draw on input from management and employees and will normally take the form of a formal report or presentation, prepared either independently or by a joint project team. High-level quantitative and qualitative analysis will examine the present strategy, financial health and operating condition of the company. For issues identified over the course of the assessment, it is important that the findings consider the severity, impact and timing of issues to determine what actions are needed.

A quick assessment should enable management to consider the following important questions:

1   Are any urgent actions required to ensure financial and operational stability? (This typically applies only to companies facing cash and liquidity issues.)

2   What are the key areas requiring management attention and focus? (This may apply to the whole company or specific business units.)

3   Should a transformation mandate be established or can issues and opportunities be managed through refocusing business-as-usual efforts?

4   Is capital available to fund changes or are short-term actions required to free up capital and create a funding pathway? (These might relate, for example, to revenue, operating margin and asset efficiency initiatives that have short-term impact.)

Assess current situation

For companies whose profitability or liquidity is an underlying concern, assessment of the current situation is primarily focused on financial issues to determine whether the company *can and should be saved*. Assessing the feasibility and likelihood of success for a financial turnaround considers three primary areas: (1) the viability of one or more core businesses, (2) adequate cash or access to bridging loans, and (3) whether organisational resources are available to drive performance improvements. In the most severe cases, the sale of the company to a strategic buyer or a controlled wind-down may be the best course of action. Otherwise a rapid and sustained focus on cash management may sustain the company in the short term while a more strategic response can be developed.

If the focus of the transformation is to realign the company for profitability, or build on existing success, a diagnostic should start with a broad assessment. This should involve looking at overall strategic, financial and operational performance across the company and assessing financial statement trends, financial metrics and ratios. More detail can be added by looking at individual business units to understand their relative performance and contribution to overall performance. More granular detail can be extracted by looking at operating performance trends and metrics within the business units or by examining specific regions, activities or products.

The output of a diagnostic should include concrete conclusions about which areas of the company require management attention and why, and outline a response plan. This plan should include a general identification of the issues and type of response required. It should identify and recommend any short-term actions that will, for example, capture 'quick wins' or address urgent operational or financial concerns. It should also identify an approach and key next steps to lay the groundwork for the development of a strategic response to fully address the challenges and opportunities faced by the company. For a step-by-step approach to undertaking a diagnostic, refer to Appendix I: Diagnosing company performance.

Ensure near-term funding

A transformation usually aims to be self-funding. Once the transformation is underway a portion of the cost savings and revenue generated by initiatives can be reinvested to fund further efforts. However, establishing a virtuous cycle often means that seed capital is needed at the outset to finance key roles and get activity underway. These funds are needed to create the mandate and drive the 'quick wins' that will lay a foundation and build traction so the transformation can progress to a stage where results will fuel ongoing delivery.

Early access to capital will be needed to drive rapid results. It is therefore important to focus on levers that can release funding quickly (typically 3 to 12 months). For financially healthy companies, an initial budget and organisational resources may be readily available. There may be cash reserves to draw on or budgets that can be reallocated. If a company is less healthy and facing a 'cash squeeze', some short-term actions may be necessary to get started (see figure 1.1, overleaf). Initiatives that are particularly effective at freeing up capital in the short term include:

- *Sales* — driving short-term sales with an intensified sales push, improved pricing and reduction in discounts

- *Cost of goods sold* — procurement efficiencies from improved sourcing strategies, including consolidation and re-tendering of major contracts

- *Operating expenses* — reduction of costs through a general or targeted cost-cutting program, including overheads, fixed costs and organisational efficiencies

- *Capital investments* — optimising capital expenditures including de-scoping, deferring or cancelling planned expenditure, and selling non-core assets.

The best actions to free up capital will differ by company and context. The diagnostic can be used to indicate which levers to target. In deciding the right initiatives, consider carefully the non-financial impact of initiatives. Ideal initiatives are not only those that release significant capital, but those that can double as an *early win* or 'lighthouse' project to create momentum and build credibility with management and employees. This means the best initiatives are no-regret actions with many positive benefits and few negative impacts. They are high value and easy to execute with little or no capital outlay, and results can be easily measured and are widely visible to the organisation. Once initiatives are decided, they should be planned, implemented and tracked to ensure the benefits are swiftly realised.

Even once early funding is secured, managing capital remains an important topic throughout the lifespan of the transformation. It is therefore important to develop an early understanding of the sources and ongoing availability of funding. The cash the company generates, its existing cash reserves and its continued access to funding all have a strong bearing on what options the company can take up.

For a robust approach to managing the company's cash position, refer to Appendix II: Monitoring and improving cash flows.

Secure early wins (quick wins)

Demonstrating impact early in the life of the transformation is essential for establishing credibility. The first three months are commonly regarded as a critical window in which new and transitioning leaders and managers must prove themselves. By driving rapid results, they can both establish credibility and create momentum, and in the process generate buy-in and build the political capital to succeed in addressing the more fundamental issues and opportunities faced by the company. While quick wins are first and foremost about building credibility and creating momentum, when selected carefully they are also opportunities to unlock near-term funding to get the overall transformation underway.

An effective method of securing early wins can be outlined as follows:

1 *Establish an identity.* Have a brand or mark that can be used on internal documents, presentations and staff communications, which can be helpful for building an identity for the change agenda.

2 *Create a platform or event.* Develop an interactive full-day workshop or event designed to spark interest and create excitement while exploring major themes linked to the change agenda.

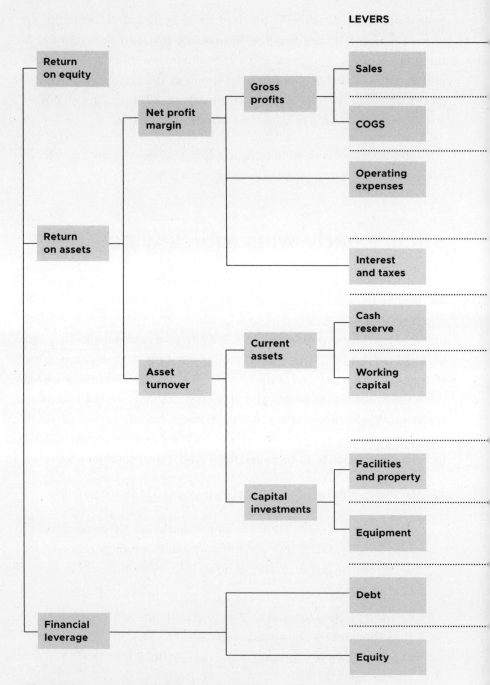

Figure 1.1: common initiatives to drive near-term improvements in cash

COMMON INITIATIVE TYPES

- Drive short-term sales

....

- Procurement efficiency initiatives
- Expense management, including austerity measures

....

- Labour efficiency (e.g. hiring freezes, compensation management and headcount reductions)
- Cost control (e.g. re-budgeting and re-prioritisation, fixed-cost reduction initiatives and overhead efficiency initiatives)

....

- Improve tax planning

....

- Improve cash management: shorten cash conversion cycle; match cash to obligations

....

- Improve inventory management (e.g. reduce materials on-hand, reduce work-in-progress, reduce finished goods inventory)
- Improve terms with trade creditors
- Improve collection terms and practices with trade debtors

....

- Non-core asset sales
- Financial structuring (e.g. sale and lease back)

....

- Capex optimisation
- Identify alternative uses for available capacity

....

- Refinance debts
- Secure near-term credit/debt facilities

....

- Optimise debt and equity
- Review dividend/share buy-back policy

3   *Win hearts and minds.* Invite a wide cross-section of staff to participate in the workshop or event, then create opportunities for attendees to participate in a project to apply workshop concepts practically.

4   *Pilot and experiment.* Establish a task force or informal project team. Seek input on potential opportunities for a pilot. This may include new opportunities identified by the task force, building on work already underway or building on earlier failed efforts. Good criteria for selecting early initiatives include opportunities that have:

   –   strong support and lead to collective wins

   –   limited potential for controversy

   –   narrow and focused scope

   –   clear benefits and value to the company

   –   little or no capital required to deliver

   –   results that can be measured (qualitatively or quantitatively)

   –   quick timelines to completion and rapid impact (less than 90 days).

5   *Execute. Execute. Execute.* Take concrete steps to implement and drive initiatives. Create routines to monitor and drive performance through to completion (such as daily stand-ups and weekly meetings).

6   *Communicate success.* Clearly track and record results, including changes in financial or operational measures, survey results or quoted stakeholder feedback, which can then be widely shared as incontrovertible evidence of success.

These activities demonstrate the process of building awareness, gathering a broad base of support by involving as many members of the organisation as possible who will work together to design and implement early wins. This approach can help shape a positive perception towards a change agenda and lay a foundation of support for the broader transformation.

Mobilise a top team

Mobilising a top team to lead and manage the transformation requires a decision on how the transformation will be organised from the outset. In its simplest form, where issues are limited to a single business unit, the best approach is often to reallocate resources and manage change through existing line staff. But in many situations, addressing the company's opportunities and issues requires a complete overhaul of the business model, including processes, roles and capabilities. This may not be easily achieved with existing line staff, since for most companies transformation is not part of the company DNA. Usually companies lack the internal capacity and know-how to design and facilitate the level of change required, so a well-coordinated and centralised approach will greatly improve the chances of success.

Centralised setup of the transformation will require management or the Board to nominate a transformation leader with overall accountability. Sometimes this responsibility is assigned to a senior executive with the best chance of driving changes forward (for example, the CEO, COO, CFO, CTO or CDO); at other times the CEO or Board will appoint an overall chief transformation officer (or some variation of this title). Deciding on the role and responsibilities of the chief transformation officer who can bring focused effort to the transformation should take account of several key questions: Will the chief transformation officer shape and run the transformation, or rather be a sounding board for the executive team? What are the current gaps? How wide should the role be? How much responsibility will they have for implementation? What profile best fits the needs of the company and its leadership team?

Every situation is different and tailoring the responsibilities of the chief transformation officer role to the company's situation should consider the severity and urgency of the issues facing the company and the effectiveness of existing management. Typical factors to consider include:

- *Types of issues.* Could the company's issues be readily resolved given greater time and resources, or are they so complex they require novel approaches with an element of risk?

- *Degree of change.* Do the company's issues relate to a single business unit, process or market, or do they span the entire company?

- *Pace of execution.* Is a quick solution needed, or can more time be afforded in return for greater certainty?

- *Degree of intervention.* Can the company manage on its own or are external resources, skills and capabilities required?

- *Degree of confidence in existing management.* Does existing management have the skills, knowledge and capabilities to deliver the change?

- *Approach to decision making.* Will key decisions be made by business units, or will they be made top-down by a select few?

Typically, the role of the chief transformation officer will correspond with one of three approaches, which differ by scope, activities and responsibility. A simple framework for evaluating which category is best suited to a situation is outlined in figure 1.2, and an explanation of each category follows.

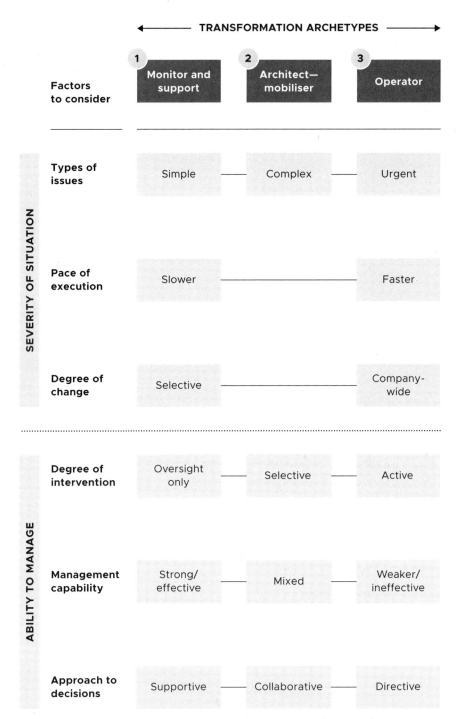

Figure 1.2: choosing how to organise for transformation

1. Monitor and support

Provide the executive team with an overall strategic framework for transformation, act as a source of advice and provide independent monitoring (see figure 1.3):

- Provide independent monitoring of delivery progress, financial impact and results; intervene in delivery by exception.

- Provide executive team with strategic framework for transformation and source of advice.

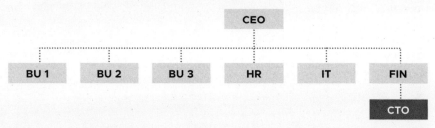

Figure 1.3: organising to monitor and support the organisation

2. Architect–mobiliser

Support the CEO and executive team with transformation planning and initiative design; provide hands-on management of delivery with varying degrees of accountability and involvement (see figure 1.4):

- Support CEO and executive team with transformation planning and initiative design:
    - jointly develop initiatives
    - validate logic.
- 'Hands-on' management of delivery (range of options):
    - lead major/cross-functional initiatives
    - actively involved in supporting delivery
    - intervene by exception.

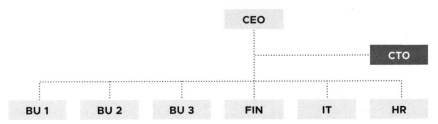

Figure 1.4: organising to architect and mobilise the transformation

3. Operator

Run the internal company operations, or key divisions within the company, and make financial and operating decisions (see figure 1.5):

- Run the internal company operations; initiate and lead transformation; make financial and operating decisions.

- Suits financial turnaround, smaller organisations and family-owned companies.

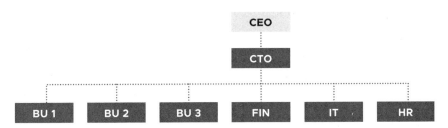

Figure 1.5: organising to operate the transformation

In addition to nominating a chief transformation officer, a central team with the right capabilities will need to be formed to provide adequate resources and skills towards a transformation. While the size, composition and skills of the central team will evolve over the course of the transformation journey, the initial focus for building a team should be on selecting key individuals who can provide early leadership and establish beneficial networks and relationships in the company. The team should be staffed with people who have the authority, credibility and skills to manage the issues faced within the company. The team should ideally represent a broad mix, drawing on current employees with a strong track record who understand the company culture, can open doors with their existing network and know how to get things done; experienced new hires who can bring outside knowledge, expertise and thought leadership; and contractors and specialists who can overcome short-term capacity constraints and address skill shortages to act quickly.

The primary aim when designing the structure of the central team and determining roles and responsibilities is to build a team that can overcome the early barriers to successful transformation by, for example, establishing or bolstering company capabilities needed to move forward in key areas such as business strategy and analysis, financial management and reporting; facilitating execution of quick wins or stabilisation initiatives; planning the transformation journey; and securing and maintaining buy-in for change. In deciding on the team structure and reporting lines, two options to consider are: a resource pool structure, typically organised around functional skills; or a matrix structure that interfaces the central team into the existing structure of the organisation (see figure 1.6).

In recent years, agile-based approaches to organising teams and delivery have become increasingly popular. An agile-based approach to delivery draws inspiration from agile software development principles to establish self-organising teams operating under agile principles and methods.[1] When setting up an agile team, ways of working are more important than the formal structure. The key components of a transformation program remain relevant to both agile and traditional delivery methods (that is, a Steering Committee for governance and a centralised transformation office to coordinate initiative teams).

Agile concepts can be readily applied to either a resource pool structure or a matrix structure to enhance delivery effectiveness. However, the adoption of agile principles can mean that formal reporting lines are less relevant.

RESOURCE POOL

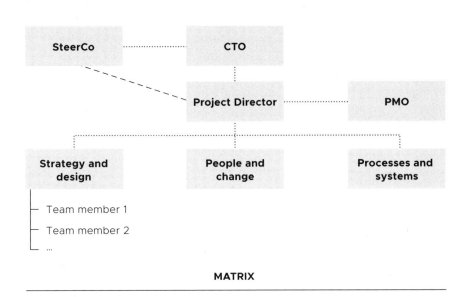

MATRIX

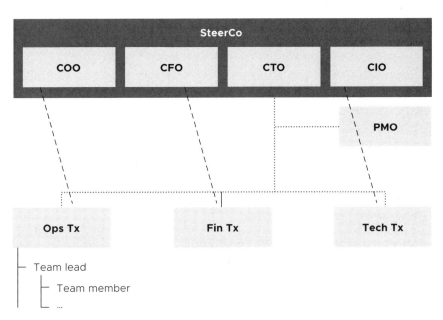

Figure 1.6: options for structuring the transformation team

The centre plays a smaller role in delivery as initiative teams are more self-directed, but the centre plays a greater role in resource management. Delivery roles are constructed to conform to the agile concepts of 'Product Owner'[2], 'Scrum Master'[3] and 'Team Members'[4], and agile ways of working, such as having daily stand-ups, sprints and regular reviews.

In choosing between different options for structuring and organising the central team (or a hybrid), there is no 'right' path, as each option has strengths and weaknesses. Making design choices and choosing between agile and traditional approaches to delivery involve trade-offs, but both resource pool and matrix structures can serve as a good starting point from which a transformation can begin. In general, pure-play structures offer a strong starting point. They can then be adapted to the realities of the organisation and individuals involved. In deciding on the right structure and roles, it is useful to consider what tailoring and adaptations will be required to cope with organisational realities. Adaptations may be needed to accommodate existing power structures, specific individuals or organisational needs. Transformational leaders can deploy a range of hybrid structures and governance models to achieve their goals. Regardless of the structure of the central team, the success of the transformation unit depends very much on the talent and capability of the individuals involved and the ability to develop a cooperative, high-performing unit with aligned goals.

SUGGESTED **ACTIONS**

1. Assess current situation

Δ   Form an initial view of the issues, supported by the facts, which identify where to focus effort and what actions are required.

Δ   Prepare some form of diagnostic, report or presentation that outlines what areas require management attention and why, and what the proposed response should be.

Δ   Gain Board or management support for the diagnostic, report or presentation, and recommendations.

2. Ensure near-term funding

Δ   Identify a source of funding to plan and implement near-term actions (such as a company budget or actions to free up capital).

3. Secure early wins (quick wins)

Δ   Develop an impactful identity or brand that creates a connection between stakeholders and the transformation.

Δ   Implement one or two small initiatives that are relatively easy to deliver and widely visible, and that build credibility.

4. Mobilise a top team

Δ   Consider how to position yourself and your team to transform the organisation, including the role and scope of the transformation leader, direct reports and team structure.

Δ   Fill select roles in a transformation team that provide the capabilities, resources and skills the organisation needs in order to transform.

Further reading

Agile Manifesto (2001). *Principles behind the Agile Manifesto* [online].

Scaled Agile (2018). SAFe® 4.6 Introduction: Overview of the Scaled Agile Framework® for Lean Enterprises [online].

Watkins, M. (2006). *The First 90 Days: Critical Success Strategies for New Leaders at All Levels*. Harvard Business Review Press.

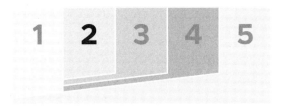

Create the mandate

At the beginning of a transformation journey, critical mass of support for change is essential; internal inertia can result in early failure. If a company is highly motivated and ready to change, finding support and legitimacy for a transformation agenda can be as simple as a CEO or top management team mandating for change and appointing a Steering Committee (SteerCo). The SteerCo can initiate the change agenda and provide overall sponsorship, direction setting and governance and this can be enough to enable the transformation planning to move forward. If a company is less ready, a more proactive engagement with executives and employees may be needed to build a support base. This may involve campaigning to secure initial interest and to obtain individual commitments. The first move might be to involve key influencers and opinion leaders.

When forming a guiding coalition to sponsor and drive early efforts to develop the transformation agenda, whether it be a formal structure such as a SteerCo or an informal network, it is important to build a broad base of support for the transformation. A strong foundation should involve enough key executives that progress won't be blocked. In addition to sponsoring executives, the taskforce should seek the involvement of individuals who have credibility with management and employees because they will have the capacity to introduce new points of view as they guide and shape the direction of the company. This active involvement by top management and an influential group of employees is pivotal to building deep levels of support for a transformation agenda.

Support for change rarely starts with everyone's cooperation. Responses are frequently mixed — from antagonists to passive participants and supporters to active champions — and while this is to be expected, a critical mass of support will be needed. Reaching sufficient buy-in can take time and can be achieved with a combination of 'hard' and 'soft' measures. Hard measures include decisions about structure and processes — such as adapting roles, responsibilities and reporting lines or replacing key management positions that are inhibiting change or blocking the change agenda. Soft measures include coaching and skills-building to promote shifts in mindsets, gathering support from key opinion leaders, and frequent discussions to reinforce the urgency and importance of a common change agenda.

Once the SteerCo or taskforce is formed, the members of the group need to establish a common view on *where the company is today, what the future outlook is* and, importantly, *why change is needed*. An effective approach for creating consensus is to develop a 'fact base' that builds on the recommendations of the initial diagnostic. The process of building the fact base needs to result in a shared understanding of the root cause of the challenges, the scope of the opportunities facing the company and how this is likely to evolve given both the internal and external contexts in which the company operates.

The process through which the fact base is developed will ensure regular and ongoing engagement among the group with opportunities for input and the incorporation of feedback. This will result in a deep shared understanding of the situation faced by the company.

Development of the fact base often follows a structured process over weeks or months. The output typically forms the basis of Board paper(s) and presentation(s), supported by an underlying financial model, that can become a useful shared point of reference for management workshops designed to envision the future and explore strategic choices. A complete fact base should provide a robust understanding of the company's current performance together with potential gaps and opportunities. These will lead to an integrated view of what is known in terms of expected future performance and what will have an impact on the company's value over time. This will be the basis for further workshops and discussions to guide the definition of a clear transformation strategy and agenda aimed at unlocking the company's full potential.

Understand the current situation

An understanding of the current situation should consider five main areas:

- *Recent performance.* This involves comparing actual and budgeted revenue, operating costs and earnings before interest and taxes (EBIT), and understanding how the company as a whole has performed in recent years, including whether it is achieving its budget targets, and the overall trend.

- *Business unit contributions.* Many companies are managed as separate parts organised by, for example, geographies, products or segments. Sometimes these parts are referred to as, for example, business units (BUs) or lines of business (LOBs). Recent performance should be disaggregated in order to understand which parts are responsible for the company's overall performance and how this has changed. Typically, this should look at changes in revenue (by organising concept) and understand the reasons for those changes.

- *Cost evolution.* Look at how the company's cost structure has evolved over time (fixed vs variable) and seek to understand what is driving this change. Understanding how the company's cost structure is evolving, and in which areas, can reveal the economics of the business and provide insight into, for example, what costs remain if volumes decline and where upward cost pressures occur.

- *Benchmarking.* An evaluation of key measures of performance of peers and comparable organisations can identify gaps between performance and best practice. Common benchmarks include cost, staff productivity and quality measures. Companies such as Gartner and the American Productivity and Quality Center (APQC) provide on-demand paid access to benchmark data companies can use to compare and evaluate performance.

- *Existing management plans.* In response to current challenges and opportunities, existing plans may already be in development or underway. Building a clear picture of the current situation involves understanding what initiatives are planned or already begun, the timing and sequence of these, and their likely impact on the company's performance.

A review of each of these five areas should be included in a robust fact base. The output and key conclusions are typically captured in charts and analyses. The illustrative output provided in figures 2.1 to 2.4 summarises recent performance, BU contributions, an evolution of costs, and benchmarking according to peers. These summary charts are typically supported with more detail on each part of the company to develop a clear understanding of what drives performance in each area and the major issues, trends and opportunities.

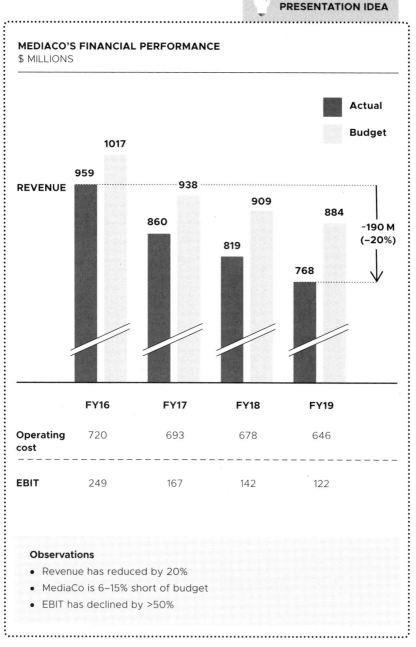

Figure 2.1: understanding the current situation — recent performance

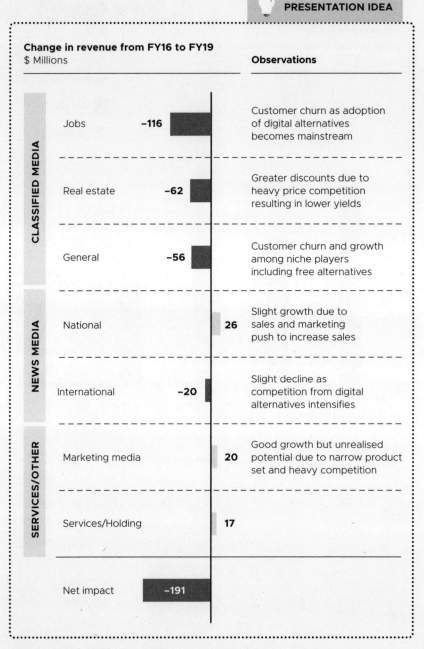

PRESENTATION IDEA

Change in revenue from FY16 to FY19
$ Millions

Observations

CLASSIFIED MEDIA	Jobs	**−116**	Customer churn as adoption of digital alternatives becomes mainstream
	Real estate	**−62**	Greater discounts due to heavy price competition resulting in lower yields
	General	**−56**	Customer churn and growth among niche players including free alternatives
NEWS MEDIA	National	**26**	Slight growth due to sales and marketing push to increase sales
	International	**−20**	Slight decline as competition from digital alternatives intensifies
SERVICES/OTHER	Marketing media	**20**	Good growth but unrealised potential due to narrow product set and heavy competition
	Services/Holding	**17**	
	Net impact	**−191**	

Figure 2.2: understanding the current situation—BU contributions

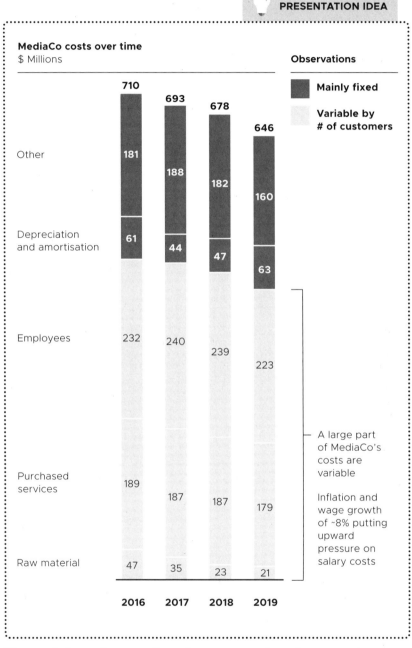

MediaCo costs over time
$ Millions

Observations

■ **Mainly fixed**

☐ **Variable by # of customers**

Category	2016	2017	2018	2019
Total	710	693	678	646
Other	181	188	182	160
Depreciation and amortisation	61	44	47	63
Employees	232	240	239	223
Purchased services	189	187	187	179
Raw material	47	35	23	21

— A large part of MediaCo's costs are variable

Inflation and wage growth of ~8% putting upward pressure on salary costs

Figure 2.3: understanding the current situation — cost structure evolution

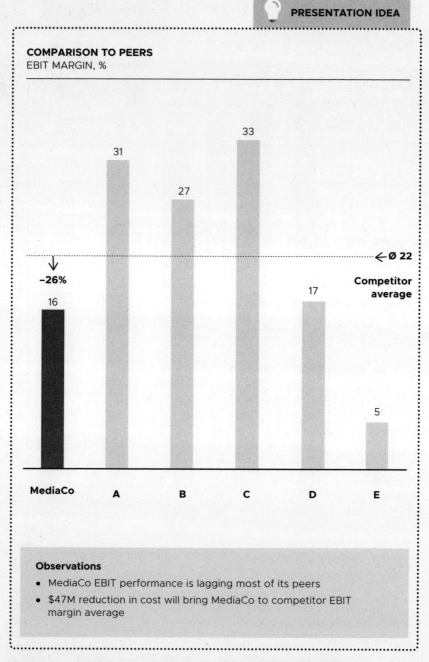

Figure 2.4: understanding the current situation—benchmarking

Determine external outlook

Current and future financial performance for many companies is heavily shaped by external factors. A company's ability to extract profits can therefore be accelerated or slowed by external shocks such as changes in customer preferences, technology breakthroughs and regulation, by the structure of the industry and by the conduct of competitors.[5] Some external conditions become tailwinds that accelerate the company's performance; others are headwinds that make future performance more difficult. Crosswinds depend largely on how management chooses to respond. As companies face a changing external outlook it's the key decisions made by management about how the company will adapt that will ultimately determine success. Development of the fact base should consider how the external environment affects the company's performance and how this is likely to change. Typical questions to consider include the following:

- What is the size of the market in which the company plays?

- Which parts of the market, or activities along the value chain, are growing and which are shrinking?

- What is the company's position in the market relative to the competition? Is it one of the pack, a challenger or a market leader?

- How has the company's market share changed over time? Who is doing well, and who is doing poorly?

- How do players in the market compare on different measures of performance (for example, top-line revenue, costs and margin)?

- What are the key market — primarily customer — trends that present challenges or opportunities, and what impact are they likely to have on the company?

- What political or regulatory changes are likely to take place in the near future and how might they affect the company?

- Are there any case study examples of successes and failures by companies facing a similar market situation?

Changes to the external environment in which the company operates can present a favourable, unfavourable or mixed impact on the current trajectory of the company. Generally, the aim should be to identify only the major external influences, and to evaluate the implication of these on each of the key financial drivers of the company's financial performance. Being able to identify those factors that present the greatest challenges and opportunities can provide a useful context for developing the transformation strategy and plans and input into forecasts, including market sensitivities and assumptions.

INTERVIEW: MICHAEL PRATT AM
UNDERSTANDING
THE CURRENT SITUATION

In early 2013, the New South Wales (NSW) government operated numerous agencies, each with responsibility for delivering a discrete set of state government services. Facing extremely low customer satisfaction scores with high levels of complaints and increasing costs-to-serve, the NSW government consolidated multiple agencies into a single cluster to form 'ServiceNSW' with the objective of establishing a one-stop shop for state government services.

Michael Pratt AM, a former banking industry CEO, was selected to oversee and transform the newly formed agency. Michael led the public body through a period of unprecedented change and ServiceNSW emerged as a global leader in the digital delivery of government services. In a few short years, customer satisfaction scores had improved from 60 per cent to 95+ per cent, costs-to-serve were considerably lower and ServiceNSW had become a globally recognised success story.[6]

Despite never having previously worked in government and faced with complex and long-standing challenges, Michael formed a deep understanding of the situation faced by ServiceNSW and a clear rationale for why change was needed. Building this foundation enabled him and his management team to develop a vision, set the strategy and put in place a multi-year roadmap for ServiceNSW from which they were able to drive exceptional results.

How did you take stock of the current situation before embarking on the transformation?

Understanding the environment and context and establishing a robust fact base were critical. In taking on my role with ServiceNSW, the first thing I did was spend six months understanding the context and situation. I set up a research lab and had many people give different advice. I wanted to understand how government worked first, and importantly what the research said citizens wanted, and I looked at external case studies of what had been done elsewhere.

How did you use an understanding of current performance and external trends to create a mandate for change?

Case studies and research were really important. Searching for and finding 25 global case studies helped us to understand what had already been tried, what worked, and what had failed elsewhere. It was very important to understand what citizens wanted. When key ministers couldn't agree, research played an important role in reaching the right decisions. It was not what I or others thought but what the citizens said that mattered.

Evaluate company impacts and base case

The emerging case for change may draw attention to performance shortfalls or perhaps to a clear opportunity to act on. In both cases, to catalyse the need for change it is important to have a clear picture of the financial and non-financial consequences of running the company based on its existing condition. Being able to develop financial projections (that is, a financial model) to estimate the company's future financial position and quantify the impact on shareholder value, EBIT or other measures of value, is essential to understanding the current state of the company and to setting a frame of reference to explore future possibilities. When an objective multi-year outlook points to a shortfall in expected earnings or an accelerating decline is forecast, this not only underpins the case for change but also helps to quantify the value at stake and the timeframe within which the company needs to respond.

Financial projections should typically span a five- or ten-year horizon. They should bring together the key insights that will have been gathered to understand the current situation and to determine the external outlook, in order to provide an integrated view of the company's performance and key operating metrics into the future. A completed financial model would typically generate a baseline or base case forecast balance sheet and P&L line items, along with key financial ratios or performance indicators. The financial model should forecast only the impact of organic growth and be built up based on existing business positions since the financial impact of mergers, acquisitions and divestitures can often be difficult to integrate and to forecast reliably. Should the company be comprised of multiple LOBs, BUs or different business models, it will usually be necessary to model each of these separately. In selecting growth rates it is ideal to choose midpoint assumptions in order to develop a baseline rather than optimistic or pessimistic choices.

Once a base case forecast model has been developed, the baseline becomes an important tool in supporting management decision making and can be used for a variety of purposes, including planning, budgeting and target setting. It is common to use the forecast model to evaluate economic sensitivities by conducting an impact assessment. This involves testing the sensitivity of changes to key drivers (such as price, customer volumes and changes in input costs) on the company's overall performance, in order to identify and prioritise the aspects of the company's business model that are most critical to future success. It may be useful to develop alternative scenarios to simulate how the company will perform under different conditions. This can be particularly useful for forecasting and planning in uncertain markets.

Figure 2.5 (overleaf) provides a simple, robust approach for building a forecast model and follows five key steps:

1   *Gather raw data.* The company's current financials provide a starting point for building a forecast model. Other relevant raw data will include market data and operating metrics. Some companies may have an existing financial model and base case, such as a long-range plan (LRP) used for budgeting, planning and forecasting that can be reused or 'flexed' based on new inputs and assumptions. In other cases, it is necessary to build the financial model from scratch, based on the available raw data and inputs.

2   *Disaggregate into lines of business.* The financial statements need to be split out into the key business drivers and the model should identify the key levers that affect the company's overall financial performance. A complex business may be made up of many different BU, categories or parts that are managed separately — geographies, products and segments, for example — which are then disaggregated into different modules, each with its own drivers and levers, to provide a more granular approach to understanding the company's performance.

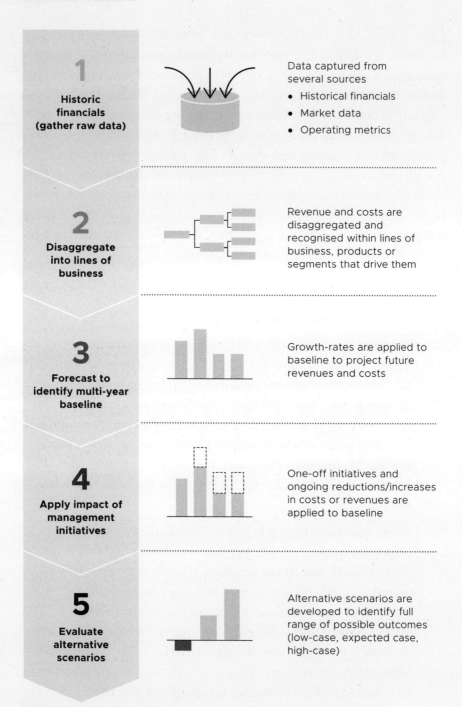

1

Historic financials (gather raw data)

Data captured from several sources
- Historical financials
- Market data
- Operating metrics

2

Disaggregate into lines of business

Revenue and costs are disaggregated and recognised within lines of business, products or segments that drive them

3

Forecast to identify multi-year baseline

Growth-rates are applied to baseline to project future revenues and costs

4

Apply impact of management initiatives

One-off initiatives and ongoing reductions/increases in costs or revenues are applied to baseline

5

Evaluate alternative scenarios

Alternative scenarios are developed to identify full range of possible outcomes (low-case, expected case, high-case)

Figure 2.5: schematic for developing a forecast model

3   *Forecast to identify multi-year baseline.* Forecast growth rates are applied to the baseline drivers and levers to project future revenues and costs. Typical inputs for determining growth rates may include the company's historical performance trends and assumptions about the market. There are many forecasting techniques, and the right approach can differ depending on the context of what is being forecast and the accuracy required.

4   *Apply impact of currently planned management initiatives.* Where there are management initiatives to respond to current opportunities or issues that would have a significant impact but that are not already included in the baseline or implied in the forecast growth rates, their financial impact needs to be applied to the baseline and forecast.

5   *Evaluate alternative scenarios (optional).* Alternative scenarios can be developed to test the current strategy under different conditions or to reflect uncertainties and inherent risks in either the company's business model or the market in which the company operates (such as high/low/expected). Market variables might, for example, decide the corridor of outcomes to determine potential results under different market scenarios.

A robust forecast model is not only the key to establishing a view on the future financial performance of the company; it is an essential tool for planning and understanding the impact of decisions throughout the transformation. In the early stages, however, the forecast model should be used to:

- establish an objective estimate of the company's financial position and the value of the company at a future date

- provide insights and highlight the evolution of the business based on changes of key business drivers

- identify which parts of the business are forecast to grow or deteriorate and the likely timeframe

- provide a tool to assess how sensitive the company's performance is to key assumptions and to evaluate the future yearly impacts of alternative scenarios

- provide management with a dashboard to inform quarterly and annual targets, set key performance indicators (KPIs) and manage against them

- estimate cash flow availability to fund investments and growth opportunities

- serve as input into workshops with the management team and to guide management towards defining the strategy that will unlock the full potential of the company.

Presenting the results of the forecast model and incorporating this into the fact base typically utilises forecast charts (see figure 2.6), and can include a clear explanation of model assumptions and comparisons between alternative scenarios (see figure 2.7, overleaf). Often each BU will have its own module or set of assumptions that together will form a company-wide view. Together these charts provide a solid basis from which to evaluate the financial impact of strategic choices and management interventions, explored in the subsequent step, to turn around or boost the company's expected future performance.

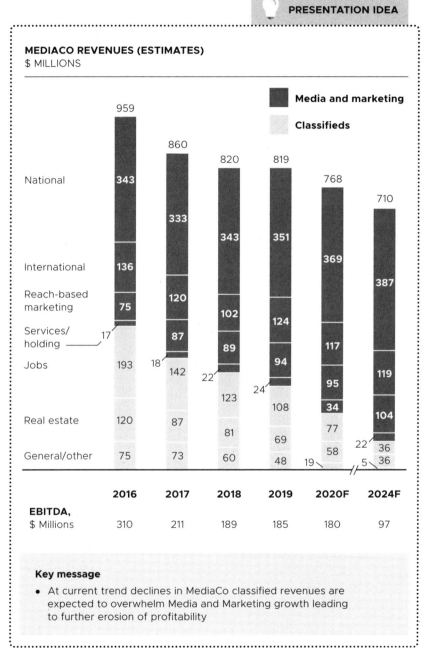

MEDIACO REVENUES (ESTIMATES)
$ MILLIONS

■ Media and marketing
□ Classifieds

959
860
820
819
768
710

National 343
333
343 351
369
387

International 136
International 136
Reach-based marketing 75
120
102
124
369
387

Services/holding 17
87
89
117
119

Jobs 193
18
142
22
94
95
119

123
24
108
34
104

Real estate 120
87
81
69
77
58
22
36

General/other 75
73
60
48
19
5
36

	2016	2017	2018	2019	2020F	2024F
EBITDA, $ Millions	310	211	189	185	180	97

Key message
- At current trend declines in MediaCo classified revenues are expected to overwhelm Media and Marketing growth leading to further erosion of profitability

Figure 2.6: object multi-year company outlook (base case only)

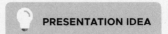

ANNUAL EVOLUTION
PERCENTAGE, %

	Low case	Expected	High case
BASE CASE FORECAST			
Sales	0%	2%	2%
• Price effect	−2%	−1%	−1%
• Volume effect	2%	3%	3%
COGS/unit	←————————	3%	————————→
Operating expense	←————————	3%	————————→
MANAGEMENT INITIATIVES			
Salesforce effectiveness	Realise 15% of 5% p.a. for 3 years	Realise 50% of 5% p.a. for 3 years	Realise 100% of 5% p.a. for 3 years
Organisation simplification	Realise 5% of $75M cost	Realise 10% of $75M cost	Realise 15% of $75M cost
Overhead cost efficiencies	Realise 8% of $8M cost	Realise 12% of $8M cost	Realise 20% of $8M cost

Figure 2.7: exploring model assumptions and alternative scenarios

SUGGESTED **ACTIONS**

1. Understand current situation

Develop a robust understanding of the current organisation. This should consider five specific areas:

Δ *Recent performance.* Develop an understanding of the organisation's overall performance.

Δ *Contribution of components.* Develop an understanding of what components are contributing to the organisation's performance and how these are evolving over time.

Δ *Cost structure.* Develop an understanding of how the inputs into the organisation's performance have changed over time.

Δ *Benchmarking.* Develop an understanding of how the organisation compares with like or similar organisations.

Δ *Existing management plans.* Develop an understanding of what management plans are already underway and how these are likely to impact performance.

2. Determine external outlook

Δ Develop a robust understanding of what is happening outside the company that will impact the organisation's performance (for example, market trends, competition, customer trends, political or regulatory changes).

3. Evaluate company impacts and base case

Δ Prepare a three- to five-year forecast of the organisation's performance, taking into account the organisation's current situation and external outlook.

Δ Update and maintain forecasts based on new information and prepare alternative scenarios if these are required to evaluate the impact of uncertainties.

Further reading

Chambers, J.C., Mullick, S.K., and Smith, D.D. (1971). 'How to Choose the Right Forecasting Technique.' *Harvard Business Review.*

Koller, T., Goedhart, M.H., Wessels, D., Copeland, T.E., and McKinsey and Company (2005). *Valuation: Measuring and Managing the Value of Companies* (6th edn). John Wiley & Sons.

Pignataro, P. (2013). *Financial Modeling and Valuation: A Practical Guide to Investment Banking and Private Equity*. John Wiley & Sons.

Kotter, J.P. (1995). 'Leading Change: Why Transformation Efforts Fail'. *Harvard Business Review* 73, 59–67.

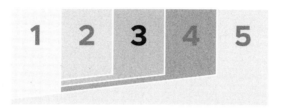

Map the journey

Setting a course to unlock the full potential of the company will require a dramatically different approach to the usual annual budget and planning exercise. The first step requires management and employees to envision and buy into an ideal future. The development of a strategy for achieving this focuses on the high-impact levers of value that will enable the company to enhance its trajectory dramatically. The company's aspirations should establish the scope and boundaries of the core business, while the strategy should identify a path towards leadership economics. Because every company is different, there is no single formula or textbook answer for what the aspirations should be, or for that matter which key strategic choices will be most effective in enabling the company to realise them; instead, the way forward must be tailored to specifically address the company's particular context, challenges and opportunities.

Developing strategic options that will enable the company to realise a bold aspiration involves 'future back' rather than 'present forward' planning to identify what key strategic decisions the management team must make in order to realise the envisioned future. Relevant strategic options that will support the company in achieving its goal may involve capturing new market opportunities, refocusing activities, building capabilities in some areas and divesting elsewhere. Rather than limit the focus of the company's strategy to a single dominant idea, the strategy should comprise a set of moves towards a common objective, leading to an integrated set of choices that work together as one coherent plan.

Major options for change should be systematically explored and evaluated in the context of the company's aspiration. Shifts may include people organisation and management, customer service, the products and services it sells, and perhaps even the markets in which it operates. The basis for change should correspond to the internal and external challenges faced to enable the company to better meet the needs of its customers and to compete more effectively with its competitors, all while giving full consideration to the company's current position, assets, and the emerging trends in the market and industry.

Once a set of strategic options has been identified, initiatives can be supported by interactive workshops and discussions to develop and generate ideas. Executed well, management workshops promote participation and strengthen engagement, which in turn builds buy-in for the transformation agenda. Workshops may lead to a wide range of strategic options and alternatives; in fact, the ideation process should result in many more ideas than can be implemented, since it necessitates making comparisons and evaluating trade-offs in order to prioritise and select the most effective choices.

Identifying the vital few strategic choices — the minimum intervention needed to achieve the transformation — involves some form of prioritisation or filtering that can be applied consistently to all options. The strategic options available to the company should be consolidated, reviewed, refined and assessed so they can be prioritised in a shortlist.

The criteria for determining importance should be the same across all options. The prioritisation process should be used to determine which strategic choices will take precedence. In practice, a common approach is to plot ideas along two axes: (1) attractiveness of choices in terms of their impact on the company's value creation targets and (2) feasibility of choices based on the company's ability to execute them. The process will indicate the areas the company must focus on, which can then be grouped and aligned to major themes to form an integrated plan that will steer the company towards its goals.

An important aspect of the strategic planning process is to assess whether the operating model is the right one and whether the organisation is in place to execute it successfully. Deciding on the right operating model involves making trade-offs in order to best organise and allocate resources within the company to execute the strategy. Identifying and designing the right operating model will presuppose considering whether current functions, capabilities, structure and accountabilities, resource levels, systems and processes, and decision-making forums are likely either to impede or to assist execution. Necessary changes to the operating model may involve hard choices about what needs to be done when and how, as well as who are the best people for particular roles. This may involve restructuring and realignment within the company.

Lastly, any definition of a new future and the strategic choices the company will make to get there need to be quantified and evaluated from a financial perspective with an eye to cash flow and funding. A clear financial plan will evaluate the financial impact of any changes to the operating model and estimate the value created from the sum of the initiatives. Overall, the way forward needs to deliver projected benefits over and above the performance baseline that underpins the case for change. Necessary adjustments may need to be made to the strategy and initiatives, including changes in sequence, timing and pace to maximise the final impact of the transformation. From a value-based management perspective, the combination of cash inflows and outflows from growth initiatives, cost optimisation and restructuring should aim to maximise overall value creation, adjusted to take account of constraints to capacity, potential risks and uncertainties.

Developing a common way forward can benefit from the creation of a comprehensive plan or strategic blueprint that has Board or top-management support. This will help consolidate the fact base and results of the strategy and planning process and formalise key decisions. In developing a strategic blueprint, strong facilitation will guide participants and decision makers towards a shared bold and ambitious set of aspirations and ensure the strategy and plan are robust, while maintaining a realistic view of the condition of the current business and the capabilities available to execute the change over the target timeframe. Achieving this balance makes defining the path ahead for a turnaround and transformation both an art and a science.

All these key activities — defining clear aspirations, building an effective strategy to support it, then selecting the priority initiatives — do not necessarily follow a linear, step-by-step process. All can involve many stakeholders, especially within large corporates, and will benefit from fact-based, insight-driven support and divergent points of view, but it's also necessary that participants come together and reach consensus on the way forward. To be effective, the company's aspirations, strategy, organisation and priority initiatives need to remain aligned and be highly congruent, so defining the path ahead will necessarily be an iterative process.

Define aspirations

A well-defined goal is a powerful signal for change and an important tool for aligning the top management team in a common purpose or objective. The process should lead to a clearly defined destination that engages people at all levels in the company and connects with them at a personal level.

Define a clear destination ...

One day Alice came to a fork in the road and saw a Cheshire cat in a tree. 'Which road do I take?' she asked. 'Where do you want to go?' Was his response. 'I don't know', Alice answered. 'Then', said the cat, 'it doesn't matter.'

Lewis Carroll

The aspiration needs to establish clearly where the company wants to be. A useful starting point from which to identify an ideal future is to develop a clear position on why the company exists — that is, its mission and purpose — then to think through the possibilities and reimagine the company unconstrained by its current realities. A company's aspiration can take different forms — a corporate vision, specific goals or benchmarks — and each of these can serve as a signpost that a major transformation is underway and establish a clear future destination.

... that involves and engages many ...

If you want to go fast, go alone. If you want to go far, go together.

African proverb

Involving the management team and extending participation to include people at all levels in the company can galvanise the organisation around a common purpose, as we all tend to be much more supportive of an agenda we helped to develop. The result is more traction and support for change than a top-down directive would achieve.

... and connects with people personally

If you want to build a ship, don't drum up the men to gather wood, divide the work and give orders. Instead, teach them to yearn for the vast and endless sea.

Antoine de Saint-Exupery

To foster buy-in for the transformation, the purpose and agenda need to connect with people at a personal and emotional level. In other words, it's about winning hearts and minds. In choosing how to frame and position the overall transformation, the use of positive emotion and drawing on employee passions can play a pivotal role in sustaining the motivation and drive for change over time. There are two main options to consider and the preferred approach may differ according to the situation:

- *Positive emotion.* Emphasise the possibilities, the opportunity to do things differently and the potential for the company to be better than it is today ('burning ambition' or a 'bold vision and opportunity'); this can suit a good to great transformation and promote the employee morale that drives a desire for change over the long term.

- *Negative emotion.* Emphasise deficiencies, the seriousness of existing shortfalls in the company and the crisis at hand — sometimes called a burning platform. This can suit an urgent crisis such as a financial turnaround because it can motivate quick action, but it may be short-lasting since a focus on deficiencies is based on fear and can lead to reduced employee engagement and increased staff turnover.

An aspiration should ideally be presented as a clear, concise, forward-looking statement that describes the ideal future for the company in an integrated way, including (1) where the company wants to be, usually in three to five years, (2) how the company will get there and (3) what the expected results will be if the company succeeds. These selected examples of companies with aspirations that incorporate these principles are drawn from company websites, company filings and other publicly available information:

OIL INDIA
(INDIAN ENERGY AND PETROLEUM COMPANY)

- **Where we are going:** Oil India 2030 vision: 'to be an international E&P [Exploration & Production] player with operations at scale in at least two geographical clusters outside India, significantly higher production, reserves and cash flows while being known globally for its capabilities to extract value from mature assets'.

- **How to get there (seven major themes):**

  » Optimise existing production locations to maximise output.

  » Expand production by developing operations in select Indian basins.

  » Set up and scale operations in one or two international markets.

  » Identify and pursue profitable adjacencies within the energy value chain.

  » Secure a top 10 ranking in global mature asset exploitation.

  » Deliver plan by restructuring the organisation, people and process.

- **What results to expect:**

  » +6–7 per cent growth p.a.

  » 50 per cent production outside Northeast India

  » among top 10 operators globally.

NEXANS
(FRENCH CABLE COMPANY)

- **Where we are going:** Nexans' ambition for 2022: 'to become a leader in advanced cabling and connectivity solutions committed to support its partners in smart energy transition, exploding data transmission and mobility'.

- **How to get there (three major themes implemented across four lines of business):**
  - » Reduce cost of operations.
  - » Invest in and strengthen core business.
  - » Pursue acquisitions and diversification.

- **What results to expect:**
  - » +5 per cent organic growth p.a.
  - » >60 per cent revenues in high-voltage, industry and telecom
  - » >15 per cent return on capital employed
  - » c. $600 million EBITDA.

BORAL
(AUSTRALIAN CONSTRUCTION MATERIALS AND BUILDING PRODUCTS SUPPLIER)

- **Where we are going:** 'Our vision is to transform Boral into a global building and construction materials company that is known for its world-leading safety performance, innovative product platform and superior returns on shareholders' funds.'

- ◆ **How to get there (key focus areas):**
  - » Capture growth in customer demand.
  - » Improve price and margin management.
  - » Increase operational efficiency to reduce costs.
- ◆ **What results to expect:**
  - » Maintain or improve market position.
  - » Offset cost increases and achieve ROI that exceeds cost of capital.
  - » 1–2 per cent savings on cost base p.a.

WINNEBAGO INDUSTRIES
(AMERICAN MANUFACTURER OF MOTOR VEHICLES)

- ◆ **Where we are going:** Winnebago 'North Star': 'We will be the trusted leader in outdoor lifestyle solutions by providing unmatched innovation, quality and service in the industries we engage.'
- ◆ **How to get there (five major themes):**
  - » Strengthen focus on leadership and accountability.
  - » Optimise and grow RV business line.
  - » Achieve best-practise operations.
  - » Innovate through digital channels.
  - » Diversify through new market exploration.
- ◆ **What results to expect:**
  - » >10 per cent market share in US
  - » >10 per cent operating income
  - » >10 per cent of revenue from new segments
  - » improved employee culture and participation.

Developing an aspiration is a creative process that involves fashioning a solution to fit the specific circumstances of the company. There is no one-size-fits-all approach. Even when two companies are very similar and face the same market conditions, the aspiration for each company may be very different. Furthermore, ownership structure and company lifecycle can also influence the aspiration and lead to very different objectives. For example, for portfolio companies an aspiration may focus on optimising resource allocation across an active portfolio to balance risk and reward. For growth companies, the focus could be on expansion along the value chain to quickly claim a new position, pursue adjacencies or meet market-share targets, while for companies with a cost-reduction imperative, the aspiration might focus on creating a time-bound, break-even position or profitability benchmark.

An aspiration should incorporate several characteristics: it should be bold, forward-looking, specific, simple, inspiring, authentic and measurable. To maximise the potency of the company's aspiration, it is worth reflecting on whether a statement of the company's aspirations embodies these key characteristics, which can help to improve the quality, content and accessibility of the aspiration:

- *Bold*. It stretches the company's ambition towards a new level of performance by targeting a challenging outcome that requires courage and resolution.

- *Forward-looking*. It focuses on where the company, market, products and customers are going to be rather than where they have been.

- *Specific*. It involves clear strategic choices about the future of the company; creates focus and lets everyone know where the company is headed; puts some stakes in the ground; and narrows the range of possibilities.

- *Simple*. It creates a communicable vision that encourages everyone to get on board, and has meaning to people at all levels in the organisation.

- *Inspiring*. It motivates and appeals by drawing on employee passions, and provides a source of meaning and purpose.

- *Authentic*. It has a credibility and substance unique to the organisation. A long-standing gap between vision and reality can create cynicism that requires renewed commitment and visible action.

- *Measurable*. It quantifies progress towards achieving the vision (objectives, clear targets). Clear objectives that underpin the vision can then help determine whether the company is on track.

Explore strategic options

To achieve the company's goal, the management team will identify what decisions and actions are required to close the gap between its present position and where it aims to be. There are often many alternative paths to realising an aspiration, though some will be less effective or certain than others. The role of a strategy is to narrow the range of options to provide a clear understanding of (1) *where* the company should compete — which markets, segments, products — and (2) *how* the company should deploy its capital, operate and be managed to better meet the needs of customers and outperform competitors. For the company's aspiration to be realised it may be necessary to capture market opportunities, reduce costs and redesign the organisation. It may also require the company to refocus, build or divest core capabilities. In this context, to develop a strategy — whether for a transformation, for a turnaround or as part of the ongoing management effort of the company — the management team will generate and fully explore the strategic options available. From among these, the team will then consider the trade-offs and commit to the strategic choices that will best enable the company to achieve its goal.

Consider the role of strategy in a market-entry example. A company assesses potential market opportunities and identifies the growing attractiveness of an adjacent market that is close to but nonetheless outside that in which the current core business operates. The strategy must determine whether this market is attractive to the company and whether the company could sustain a competitive advantage if it chose to compete there. If it is a good option, it will also be necessary to identify the best vehicle for entering this market, which could be through organic growth as the company builds the product and operations required, a partnership with another company or an acquisition of a company that already operates there. From the first-order decision about whether the company should enter the adjacent market relative to other opportunities, through to questions about how to best execute an entry decision, the company's top management team needs to form a clear view on its strategy and what strategic choices will deliver the best results.

Choosing the right strategy can lead to an enormous difference in economic outcomes. Consider the example of Kodak and Fujifilm, who faced very similar market conditions as profit pools shifted away from traditional cameras and film processing towards digital alternatives. Despite markedly similar challenges, the ultimate fate of these companies was very different. Kodak focused on major cost-cutting to preserve its profitability in a declining market, then made a late entry into the highly competitive digital photography market with limited competitive differentiation or cost leadership. Over this same period, Fujifilm adapted and explored the application of its technology in adjacent markets. They diversified, using internal know-how to find new markets where they could compete effectively. After assessing numerous alternatives, Fujifilm made a clear choice to compete by setting up Imaging Solutions, Information Solutions and Document Solutions, and established three separate operating segments to service clients in these markets.

The companies operated as close rivals in early 2000, but just over a decade later Kodak had failed, filing for bankruptcy in 2012, while Fujifilm thrived and was generating significantly more revenue than it had in the traditional camera and film processing market (see figure 3.1).

REVENUE INDEX
BASE YEAR = 2000

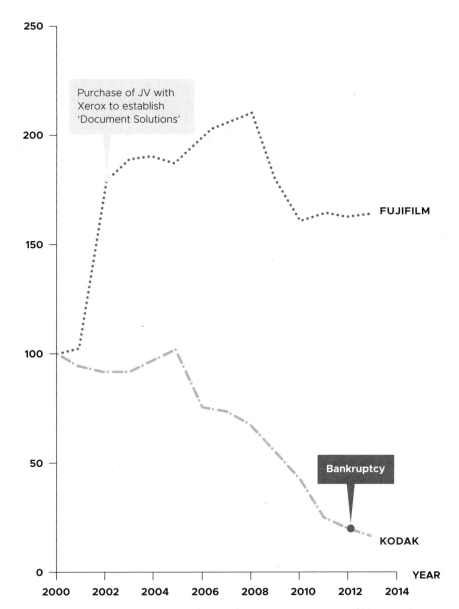

Figure 3.1: different strategic choices led to vastly different fates

Source: Based on information sourced from Fuji Photo Film Co., Ltd, U.S. Securities and Exchange Commission, Macrotrends LLC, Eastman Kodak Company.

Developing strategic options requires the generation and assessment of many ideas to capture the opportunities and best address the issues that will lead to the fulfilment of the company's goals. Some companies follow a more formal planning process in which strategy is deliberate, while for others strategy is emergent and evolves flexibly over time as the company moves towards achieving its vision. For many companies aiming for a step-change in performance, strategic choices will be required simply to get the basics right. But new breakthrough ideas that will enable the company to grow along new s-curves are also needed. Beyond obvious choices, the use of strategic frameworks, tools and approaches can assist in the development of strategic options; ultimately, though, each case is unique because it depends on the market, the company and the people involved.

Multiple tools can assist the process of generating and developing strategic options, including:

- *Prescriptive strategies.* Strategic solutions are required when a textbook problem or situation presents itself, such as when it makes sense for a company to integrate forwards or backwards along the value chain. Many private equity firms excel at searching for and identifying a textbook situation and deploying a playbook of tried and tested strategies.

- *Choice frameworks.* Tools and approaches may be used to develop options and force choices. For example, Porter's generic strategies for competing insist a management team be clear on whether it makes sense for a company to pursue cost leadership, differentiation or focus strategies in order to outperform competitors.

- *Management experience and judgement.* The role of creativity, inductive logic and lateral thinking should not be overlooked in developing strategic options.

In practice, developing strategic options involves facilitating con-versations and discussion forums that raise the necessary questions. The context of a management offsite workshop, for example, can make use of breakout sessions to ideate and brainstorm possible strategic options. Preparing a list of ideas beforehand or defining a draft strategy that hypothesises what will successfully deliver the goal can assist in getting the best results from workshop discussions. Breakout sessions and discussions should identify breakthrough themes or actions the company must commit to in order to achieve its goals or vision for the future.

To fully maximise the potential of the company, the development of strategic options for a transformation/turnaround needs to address three areas simultaneously:

1   *Existing business.* What parts of the company are core? What strategic options will ensure the core business will succeed in the short term and achieve a sustainable competitive advantage in the long term?

2   *New business.* What strategic options will enable the company to capture attractive future growth opportunities in new markets/segments/products?

3   *Linkages.* If the company comprises multiple parts, how should those parts operate together and be managed to maximise value creation?

Strategic options for driving early cost savings can provide an essential source of funding for other options and are a means of achieving sustainability and funding options focused on growing market share. Furthermore, it's very difficult for a strategy themed on cost reduction to be a source of motivation within the company. To counteract this, the strategy needs (1) to address the potential for growth and excite employees about future prospects and (2) to release cash and create the efficiencies required to fund investment priorities. Even when cost-cutting is a major theme of the strategy and is an urgent priority in the short term, a company should not rely exclusively on cost reductions, as on their own they are not sufficient to ensure long-term sustainability. Every business needs a clear long-term growth agenda. This means that even in a cost-centric transformation it's important to pursue growth options that connect a cost-reduction agenda to the top line with a future vision for the company.

To provide a source of ideas, this chapter outlines a list of strategic options categorised into three groups that could form part of a company transformation or turnaround strategy: (1) cut cost and manage profits, (2) deliver growth and (3) selectively build capability (and possibly divest). In making strategic choices, it's important to match the scale and scope of the challenges and opportunities faced by the company. While the list is by no means exhaustive, it is a starting point for ideas and further discussion.

Cut cost and manage profits

For any legacy core business facing a challenging market, especially where core segments are in structural decline and the company faces slowing single-digit core growth, it is important to be able to match market demand with a cost structure that will enable the company to operate profitably over the longer term. To adapt to new market conditions, a company may have to be able to operate profitably at lower levels of demand, and the right cost structure may be difficult or impossible to achieve by merely polishing what is already in place. A complete rethink of how the company operates and services its customers may be required. Being able to recognise this is the true value of taking a transformative approach to reducing cost.

Resetting the company's cost position involves a combination of top-down structural ideas — who performs what and where. But it also involves a bottom-up identification of opportunities — incremental ideas that evaluate the need for activities and drive improvements at a process and activity level. Combining top-down structural changes with bottom-up incremental improvements will enable the company to address the entire cost base and deliver a cost reduction from different angles. Areas of the company that have the largest addressable cost base and the greatest degree of cost compressibility are likely to offer the greatest potential benefits. Common strategic options may include:

- *Overhead cost reduction.* Reduce operating expenses by cutting budgets through targeting a percentage reduction or making longer-term improvements to selling, general and administrative expenses (SG&A) functions, and processes.

- *Strategic procurement and sourcing.* Analyse spend, review category strategies, sourcing strategies (make vs buy decisions), improve supplier management and ensure a strategic approach to consolidating, retendering and renegotiating contracts.

- *Simplify products and offers.* Redesign products based on customer value or reducing the number of stock-keeping units (SKUs) to reduce complexity and cost.

- *Drive functional or divisional cost transformation (cost efficiency program).* Reduce addressable costs by optimising a business function or set of operational activities. For example:

  - *Supply chain.* Optimise locations and distribution footprint to reduce cost/enhance service levels.

  - *Production.* Improve production outputs by eliminating waste and reducing variation.

  - *Technology.* Optimise, rationalise and consolidate platforms and infrastructure.

  - *Marketing.* Optimise marketing activities and allocation of media spend to maximise return on investment. For reduction in advertising budgets, see overhead cost reduction.

  - *Sales.* Restructure sales organisation and performance management. For salesforce effectiveness, see focus on existing business growth.

- *Re-engineer and/or digitise processes.* Reduce cost and improve productivity by re-engineering processes; that is, eliminate non-value-added activities and combine, rearrange, simplify and standardise processes. Additionally, artificial intelligence and technology-enabled automation are increasingly being used to improve process quality and reduce labour costs.[7]

- *Outsourcing and offshoring.* Outsource capabilities, activities and functions to less costly locations, especially those that are highly transactional and have a low need for physical presence.

Deliver growth

Selection and development of growth initiatives should aim to increase the company's existing trajectory and further accelerate profitable growth. Sources of growth to explore include strategic options that maximise the profitable growth of the core business, options that draw on existing sources of advantage within the company to expand into adjacent attractive markets, and through acquisitions. Development of growth choices can benefit from dedicated resources and a systematic approach. It is often advisable that implementation of growth choices is ring-fenced or operates as a standalone business in order to incubate and protect them from the core or legacy business. Choosing the right portfolio or mix of growth options can be an important factor to consider as different configurations can result in dramatic differences in the size of the revenue impact and timing of benefits.

Growing the existing core business

Within the existing core business there may be several sources of untapped growth, which the strategy for the transformation should capitalise on. Options to grow the core business typically require less capital, involve less risk, and can be realised more quickly than opportunities outside the core business. Common strategic options may include the following:

- *Develop winning/hero products.* Create and sell innovative products (or innovate the business mode) to increase market demand or take market share from competitors.

- *Execute price increases.* Raising prices is a powerful lever for improving the company's bottom line, particularly when customer sensitivity to price changes is low.

- *Improve salesforce effectiveness.* Aim to improve sales results with a program that matches sales processes and systems, resources and capabilities to customer needs and segments.

- *Focus on pockets-of-growth.* De-average performance in the existing business and increase effort and focus on areas of the company with the highest potential by means of, for example:

  - prioritising core markets/segments/clients

  - exiting unprofitable or low-margin segments

  - improving product/customer service performance.

- *Pursue acquisitions.* Acquire and integrate a competitor or related company to increase scale or fill a capability gap.

Establishing growth from new business

Exploring sources of growth beyond the core business can overcome the natural limits imposed by the size and growth rate of the markets in which a company already competes. Strategic options that involve activities outside of the existing core business carry a greater degree of risk, but can be essential for creating the headroom for growth, if the company is to reach its aspirations. Common strategic options include:

- *Expand into adjacencies.* Offer new products in existing markets or enter new markets with existing products.

- *Expand into new geographies.* Establish a market presence in international markets.

- *Diversification.* Enter entirely new markets or develop entirely new products unrelated to core business.

- *Pursue acquisitions.* Acquire a related company to gain access to a new market or fill a capability gap.

INTERVIEW: NEIL ROBINSON
SUCCESSFUL GROWTH STRATEGIES

Neil Robinson is an accomplished sales and marketing executive with over two decades of experience in leading the growth agenda inside media, content and marketing businesses. He has led growth in both large listed corporates and innovative start-ups, overseeing existing revenue streams and employing diversification strategies to develop new and sustainable sources of revenue.

To reposition a company for growth, Neil places particular emphasis on reorganising it to promote competence, cohesion and a growth culture. When creating a growth strategy for a legacy business, Neil stresses how important it is that the company set their sights beyond short-term opportunities, and explore innovative growth and other competitive strategies to ensure sustainable performance.

Why is it important for companies to have a clearly defined strategy for growth?

Many businesses are run really well operationally, but without a dedicated focus on growth companies tend to stagnate. Over time, conservatism, limiting mindsets and inward-looking cultures can set in, and so businesses need a 'North Star' to guide growth and expansion; this moves the company from where it is today to where it needs to be.

How do you set a growth strategy that will maximise the company's trajectory?

Too often, companies limit growth potential by defining their business and ambitions solely in the present. A growth strategy should remove these limitations, and shift the focus outside of the immediate here and now. Companies need to look for growth across three horizons: today's core business; new businesses for tomorrow; and innovating and experimenting to create viable future options. This approach enables companies to take a broader view of market opportunities, and take inspiration from other industries and companies.

What factors should senior executives consider in developing successful strategies for growth?

Executives should start with an assessment of the company's growth capital. This involves looking at the company's propensity for growth and ensuring the relevant factors are in place to succeed. A mandate for growth that comes from the top is essential, and to activate the strategy throughout the organisation, companies should start by building muscle in three areas: competence, cohesion and culture. Competence is about having the right talent; cohesion is about unifying the management team to work together; and lastly companies need to foster a culture that embraces trust, learning and experimentation. All these factors come together when driving growth, and it's the companies that get this equation right that thrive.

Selectively build capability (and divest)

In exploring strategic options, compare the capabilities and assets the company holds today with those needed to succeed in the future. Recognising which capabilities will provide a true competitive advantage in the future, and investing in those, can maintain or establish a market leadership position. On the other hand, strategically reducing or divesting capabilities that contribute little value to the company now or are unlikely to add value in the future can unlock leverage capacity for the core business or provide further investment capital to fund growth options.

Capability building can be essential for building the future foundations of the company, particularly when market and customer expectations have changed dramatically. However, often the benefits of capability building cannot be easily articulated or quantified, which means they are sometimes characterised differently from other strategic options and referred to as strategic enablers. These are strategic choices that enable a company to execute the strategy and align with the aspirations and vision of the management team but are not a strategy in themselves.

The choice of which capabilities and assets the company should pursue is important, as companies are rarely able to compete effectively in all areas of their business model, and capabilities that are central to the core of the company's business can deliver a disproportionate impact on performance. It is important, then, to decide the areas of capability in which the company will be 'distinctive', 'at par' or 'below best'. For example, capital-intensive industries are more likely to benefit from building real strength in procurement or project delivery, while retailers and fast-moving consumer goods companies (FMCGs) may find that excellence in parts of their sales and marketing function is critical to their future success. Those areas of the company that are 'below best' are natural outsourcing or partnership opportunities. Strategic options to enhance or reduce the organisation's capabilities to match future requirements may include:

- *Pursue functional excellence.* Build strength/differentiation in areas that will be a source of competitive advantage in the current or future business.

- *Leverage existing assets.* Truly differentiated or unique assets such as brand or critical technology or location assets have the potential to be further enhanced or used in new ways.

- *Redesign operating model.* This may deliver some cost advantages, but it is primarily about organisational effectiveness achieved through better managing and by organising different parts of the company to drive better synergies.

- *Talent and performance management.* Create a compelling value proposition to attract and retain talent, improve hiring practices, replace low performers, retain high performers, and invest in workplace training and development.

- *Separation (of non-core assets).* Spin off or sell divisions and use the capital to resuscitate the core business or to drive a renewed focus on operating and growing the core. This may involve fixing the business and getting it ready to sell.

- *Reset culture and values.* Improving aspects of a company's culture can play an enormous role in its health and may be a key to addressing systemic issues that are affecting performance.

Determine strategic priorities

Deciding which set of strategic choices is best for the company and should form part of the overall strategy requires ruthless prioritisation. In every company and situation resources are limited — perhaps even constraining — so the company should pursue only the vital few strategic choices that are going to have the greatest impact on realising its goals. Too often a company can have multiple, and sometimes incompatible, choices about the right way forward. A winning transformation strategy is one in which strategic options are congruent, or at least not at odds with one another. It focuses the resources and effort of the organisation on what matters and limits distractions.

When prioritising strategic options or broad themes that form the basis of the transformation strategy, the aim is to identify and focus on three to five: fewer interventions are better. The power of prioritisation is that it creates a focus and allows the company to concentrate resources on the areas that matter and to act quickly. Some strategic options are going to be easier to implement than others and will generate a greater return and present a better fit with the overall vision — so prioritisation is key to maximising benefits. The process of prioritisation demands clear criteria that can be applied consistently across all choices, as well as involving the right decision makers. Common criteria include ease of implementation and financial impact. However, a prioritisation activity should emphasise people over process: Common approaches for comparing options and prioritisation include:

- *2 × 2 matrix*. Identify the two critical dimensions on which to score each strategic option and prioritise 'top quadrant' initiative (see figure 3.2).

- *Multi-criteria filters*. Filter all strategic options through a series of either objective or subjective criteria to identify a prioritised subset (see figure 3.3, overleaf).

- *Scorecard*. Score all initiatives based on criteria that can include many dimensions and sum results. Use a scale or Harvey Balls (see figures 3.4 and 3.5, pp. 65–66).

- *Survey*. Send participants a survey to score or rank initiatives based on criteria, and aggregate the results to determine priorities.

The company's strategic priorities should be based on the robust assessment of each option's impact on the P&L and balance sheet. This may require further development of strategic options and clarification of the underlying initiatives to provide the necessary detail to support a final decision. For initial direction setting, a top-down and qualitative approach is well suited to screening options, while a bottom-up approach can be used for further validation. In general, the objective is to gain broad support for the way ahead. The process of prioritisation will be revisited many times, not just in determining the initial priority of strategic options but to reflect changes in priorities as more information becomes available. Subsequent iterations towards the final set of strategic choices form the basis of the forward management agenda. The resulting set of strategic choices should be consolidated and incorporated into the strategic blueprint. Together these clear choices lay the path ahead and underpin the strategy for the transformation (see figure 3.6, p. 67).

Description

1. Grow retail segment

2. Rationalise locations

3. Improve risk-management capability

4. Re-engineer/digitise back-office processes

5. Reduce overhead costs

6. Simplify organisational structure

7. Enter into corporate segment

8. Activate SME segment

9. Decrease cost of liabilities

10. ...

11. ...

12. ...

Figure 3.2: use of a 2 × 2 matrix to prioritise ideas

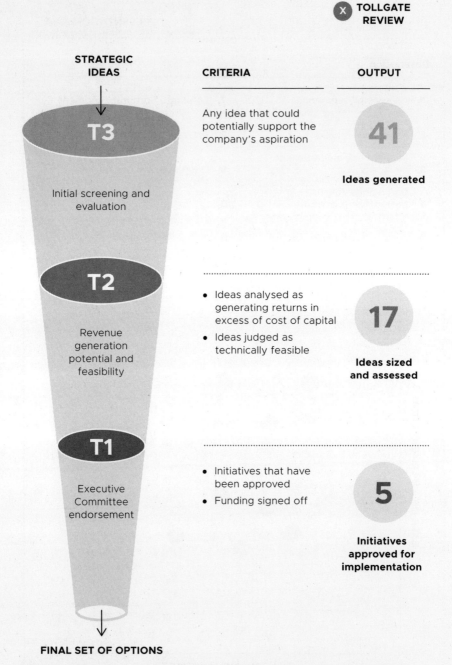

Figure 3.3: use of multiple (subjective) filtering criteria to compare ideas

		SCORE		
	1	**2**	**3**	**4**
SIZE OF OPPORTUNITY (CRITERIA 1) — **Increases revenue**	Little or no impact on revenues	Generates benefit of $2m–$5m	Generates benefit >$5m	Generates significant and sustainable revenue >$10m
Reduces cost base	Little or no impact on cost base	1–5% improvement in cost base	5–10% improvement in cost base	>10% improvement in cost base
Improves customer satisfaction	Little or no impact on customer satisfaction	Some impact on customer satisfaction within a single segment	Impact on customer satisfaction across multiple segments	Impact across all customer segments, brands and products
IMPORTANCE TO COMPANY (CRITERIA 2) — **Urgency**	Impact is the same whether undertaken in next 3–5 years or later	Opportunity within 3–5 years but likely to reoccur	Ability to capture opportunity in next 3–5 years may not reoccur	A critical window of action opening in next 1–3 years
Ease of capture	High degree of risk and uncertainty on costs, schedule and impact	Moderate degree of risk and uncertainty on costs, schedule and impact	Some risks are present but they are well understood and can be mitigated	Opportunity is familiar; can be captured with little or no risk
Builds foundations for future	Improves current capability but may not support future business needs	Builds capability to support existing business and is relevant to future	Builds capability which creates options for future expansion	Builds essential capability which preserves the 'right to play'

Figure 3.4: use of common criteria to score initiatives (1/2)

		STRATEGIC CHOICES / INITIATIVES TO SCORE											
		Option 1	Option 2	Option 3	Option 4	Option 5	Option 6	Option 7	Option 8	Option 9	Option 10	Option 11	Option 12
SIZE OF OPPORTUNITY (CRITERIA 1)	Increases revenue	2	2	2	2	0	1	3	2	2	3	3	2
	Reduces cost base	1	1	1	1	4	1	4	1	1	1	1	1
	Improves customer satisfaction	2	2	3	1	4	3	3	1	1	3	3	3
IMPORTANCE TO COMPANY (CRITERIA 2)	Urgency	2	2	2	2	4	4	3	2	2	3	3	2
	Ease of capture	2	2	2	2	2	2	3	2	2	3	4	1
	Builds foundations for future	1	1	1	1	1	1	4	2	2	4	4	3
	TOTALS	10	10	11	9	15	12	20	10	10	17	18	12

Figure 3.5: use of common criteria to score initiatives (2/2)

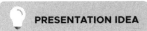

	Description	Rationale	Impact on 2018/19 profit, $Bln
1 Capture retail growth	Continue to pursue the retail segment by leveraging existing strengths for further growth	• Competitive advantage and high market share in settlements • Lacking value proposition at bank level and secure lending capabilities	9.0–10.5
2 Activate small and medium-sized businesses (SME)	• Develop segment-specific value proposition and offer • Address gaps to meet SME needs	Further increase the potential of departments engaged in SME business	0.4–0.5
3 Develop corporate segment	• Develop value proposition and revamp credit process • Enhance frontline capabilities	Expand business scope to address needs of medium-sized corporate clients	0.3–0.4
4 Improve risk management	Upgrade governance and close gaps in credit risk functions	Improve management and organisational systems to manage complex risks	**NA**
5 Manage operating expenses and organisation	• Launch program for optimising operating expenses • Improve organisational efficiency and address gaps	• Management of opex will create savings to fund initiatives • Organisational improvements is a key enabler for profitable growth	1.6–1.7
TMO	Create team to support delivery of transformation program		**TOTAL 11.0–13.0**

Figure 3.6: setting clearly defined strategic priorities

Source: Based on information taken from 'Strategy of JSC CB "PRIVATBANK" until 2022', page 30 'Transformation program relies on a clear set of initiatives that will increase2018–2019 profit of PrivatBank by ~UAH11-13 bln (1/2)' https://en.privatbank.ua/about/strategy

Develop initiatives and roadmap

For each strategic choice or strategic theme that forms part of the company's overall transformation strategy, it will be useful to further break down the strategic choice into a set of initiatives. These can then be planned in greater detail to clearly define who, how and when in terms of implementing the initiatives that underpin the strategic choice. Individual strategic choices may comprise one or many different initiatives, each with its own objective, set of activities, milestones and financial targets, and KPIs that must be achieved. Each initiative should have single-point ownership. The owner needs to be carefully selected: they will be the person with whom the primary benefit of the initiative resides, and they will have access to the right information and resources. The owner is therefore typically a sponsoring executive. In large or complex organisations, or when the content of the strategy has significant cross-functional scope, the execution of an initiative can often involve many interdependencies. It is, then, important to clarify the responsibility of individual components, including upfront identification of support roles involved in the delivery of an initiative.

As the planning and development of initiatives is undertaken, it will become clear how the strategy will decompose the strategic choices into clearly defined scope, budget and timelines. For each strategic choice, whether it comprises one or multiple initiatives, an actionable plan that captures the essential details will be required. The best way to gather the information is to establish joint teams with proposed initiative owners and Finance to systematically capture inputs in a basic template (see figure 3.7).

The purpose of gathering inputs on each initiative is to finalise the front-end concept and design of the strategy to establish high-level 'charters' with validated estimates for each initiative that will include the associated benefits, costs and timeframe for delivery. At this stage, financials are top-down- and bottom-up-validated estimates. In chapter 5, 'Set up initiatives and design detailed solutions' looks at

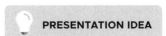

PRESENTATION IDEA

| **Initiative name** | Enhance retail value proposition | **Initiative lead** | Daniel K. |

Scope/objectives

- Retail segment represents an attractive growth opportunity that has not been properly served for a long period of time
- Introducing more competitive products, improved marketing and strengthening sales capability will enable the company to grow with the market in retail lending, which will lead to improved profitability

Metrics and targets

| Metric | Baseline | Target | | | | | | | |
| | | Year 1 | | | | Year 2 | | | |
		Q1	Q2	Q3	Q4	Q1	Q2	Q3	Q4
Lending volume, $	[x]	[x]	[x]	[x]	[x]	[x]	[x]	[x]	[x]
Net interest income %	[x]	[x]	[x]	[x]	[x]	[x]	[x]	[x]	[x]
Net commission income $	[x]	[x]	[x]	[x]	[x]	[x]	[x]	[x]	[x]
...	...	...	...	...	...	...	...	...	...
...	...	...	...	...	...	...	...	...	...
...	...	...	...	...	...	...	...	...	...
...	...	...	...	...	...	...	...	...	...

Milestones, timing and team

Milestones	Deadline	Lead	Support	Area of focus
Segment retail customers	Q3	Sarah K.	Aarav M.	Research
Conduct needs analysis	Q3	Sarah K.	Aarav M.	Research
Develop new product roadmap	Q1	Sarah K.	Aarav M.	Product
Plan and develop marketing	...	Lisa P.	...	Market
Evaluate sales channel requirements	Q2	Aarav M.	...	Sales
Roll out new sales channels (if required)	Q4	Aarav M.	...	Sales
...	...	...	...	...

Figure 3.7: templates to gather and validate initiatives

developing detailed budgets; lastly, chapter 5, 'Manage initiative delivery' turns to cost control.

Information usually captured in charter templates includes:

- *Initiative name.* Provide a short title for the initiative. Large or sensitive projects are sometimes given an internal project name.

- *Description of scope and objectives.* Provide a summary description of initiative objectives and clarifications on overall scope.

- *Single-point owner.* Include the name of the individual (for example, the sponsoring executive or general manager) who has overall accountability for ensuring that the initiative is successful.

- *Metrics and financial targets.* Include the key financial targets and operational metrics that can be used to measure the success of the initiative. This involves establishing a baseline and setting future targets. Like revenue targets, financial targets should include required operating expenses and capital outlays. Investment requirements and time to realise are important to capture so the payback period can be determined along with the P&L and balance sheet impacts (see 'Consolidate financial impact' later in this chapter).

- *Milestones and deadlines.* Identify any major activity milestones and deadlines that can be used to measure progress. Milestones can be a good lead indicator when financial benefits are 'lumpy' and don't accumulate steadily.

- *Team and accountabilities.* For any major activity, identify owners, particularly where cross-functional leaders are required to provide input, so that interdependencies are understood.

Details captured in each of the initiative templates should be consolidated into a roadmap that will provide an integrated multi-year view of all the future activities required to implement the strategy. This consolidated roadmap is a key artefact for planning and managing implementation programmatically. There are different approaches to conceptualising and managing initiatives as part of an integrated plan that can depend on the certainty of requirements and confidence in execution. For this reason, approaches for visualising the roadmap can span abstract representations such as 'transformation map' and chevron-style representations, as well as more concrete plans with timelines and milestones (Gantt charts) (see figures 3.8 and 3.9, overleaf). Many companies choose to manage initiatives relating to each strategic choice dynamically as a portfolio instead of serially executed initiatives. This ensures high-level planning remains fluid so that delivery can be adapted to respond to unexpected challenges and opportunities.

During the initial stages of developing the roadmap, scheduling should take place at a high level and should ignore the specific details of each initiative. Getting into detailed planning doesn't buy any advantages in the early stages, although it is often useful to explicitly split the allocation of time to highlight the duration to be set aside for planning and implementing each initiative. The purpose of the roadmap is to outline the overall logic of the program and to establish the ideal sequence and pace of the implementation. It should create a sense of how compressed the delivery plan is overall, and whether there is too much or too little activity in specific areas. When deciding the initial sequence and timeframe for delivery, common principles or criteria can be applied to enhance financial benefits, minimise change efforts and mitigate delivery risk, and these should be factored into the design of the roadmap. They may include:

- *Momentum.* Prioritise at least one or two visible early wins that can be implemented almost immediately. Even if the results are not financially outstanding, they will motivate further change.

- *Funding profile.* Sequencing of initiatives should aim to capture financial benefits as quickly as possible; if fast payback initiatives are prioritised, results can be reinvested and upfront investment minimised; this is particularly important when funding is a constraint.

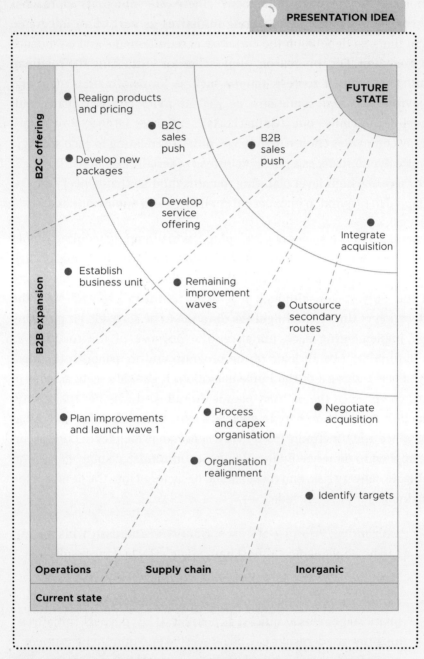

Figure 3.8: roadmap for implementing strategic choices (transformation map)

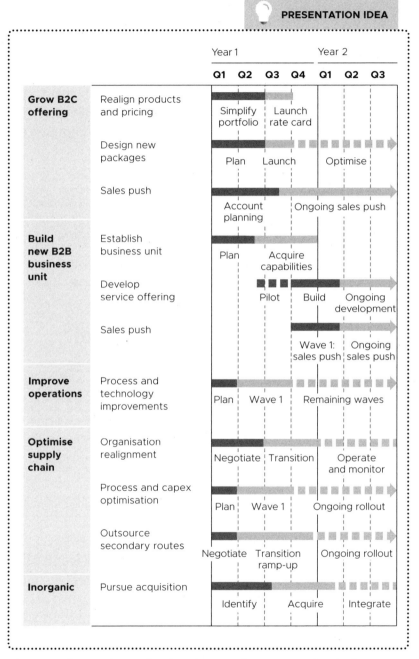

PRESENTATION IDEA

Figure 3.9: roadmap for implementing strategic choices (Gantt chart)

- *Cohesiveness.* Scheduling of initiatives should work together so the result is greater than the sum of its parts. Initiatives that enable other initiatives or are on the critical path should be started early and prioritised so they don't become bottlenecks.

- *Change effort.* The capacity to absorb change in any company is limited, so the implementation plan will need to balance the intensity, duration and frequency of major change to minimise its disruption and avoid fatigue. Decisions about how much pressure to put on the system should be factored into scheduling.

- *Agility.* Robust plans are responsive and able to deal with challenges and opportunities as they arise. The overall schedule should be managed as a portfolio that can accommodate changes to the schedule alongside existing priorities. This will enable short-term victories without losing sight of the three- to five-year aspiration.

Outline future operating model and organisation

A prerequisite for implementing the strategy and initiatives is having the right operating model in place. Simply put, the operating model sets out how the company is managed and organised in order to create value for its end customer. To deliver the transformation, the company will have in place a combination of the right functions, capabilities, structures, roles and accountabilities, resource levels, systems and processes, and decision-making forums. All of these will need to work together cohesively for the strategy to be implemented and the organisation to operate like a well-oiled machine. In this context, particularly when organisations are underperforming, realigning the company's operating model with the strategy and the roadmap, while also addressing barriers to organisational effectiveness, is an integral part of driving a step-change in productivity and efficiency.

The future operating model will be based on the company's aspirations and strategy. This means any elements in the model that are likely to inhibit the strategy, or potential gaps and bottlenecks, will need to be identified and addressed to ensure a successful transformation. There is no perfect operating model, and in the first instance the focus of changes should be isolated to the essential shifts necessary to implement the strategy. Different design choices can dramatically reshape the organisation's strengths and weaknesses, but just because changes can be made doesn't mean they should be. Only make major changes if there is a strong case to do so; and limit their number because too many changes can disrupt the operating model. Commit to a primary organising concept first, and undertake major changes only if the benefits are clearly understood and the company is confident they can be executed.

Implementing changes to the operating model can be a significant challenge, not only because realising the full benefits of major operating model redesign can take 12 to 18 months or even longer, but also because strong senior management support is essential. Like any decision that has the potential for zero-sum results, operating model changes can be met with resistance and require difficult trade-offs and hard choices. Major realignment of the operating model can be treated as a major strategic initiative in itself, but from a transformation-delivery perspective, the scope can be narrowed to focus on only the 'enablers', or changes required to implement the strategy. The process for defining a future operating model can follow a structured, fact-based approach. Gathering relevant information can involve deep, structured interviews, use of staff surveys, and human resources (HR) data analysis. It's important to test the impact of design decisions and get firsthand input from staff; workshopping the operating model design can achieve this.

Determine operating model requirements

We recommend a step-by-step approach to designing the future operating model. Start by determining a set of design principles to establish the target state operating model. Principles should be few and simple, follow organisational design best practice and be based on the company's strategy. Operating principles will articulate what is important. Specific priorities that are part of the strategy might include cost targets, critical capabilities, growth focus and customer focus. Typical criteria for applying these priorities include avoiding duplication, developing expertise in key areas, capturing economies of scale and enabling customer responsiveness. Sometimes operating model design principles can be at odds, as is the case, for example, when customer responsiveness is set against cost effectiveness. It can be useful to force rank principles to arrive at the final set. Table 3.1 offers an example of key operating model principles that balance organisational aspirations and constraints.

Table 3.1: illustrative operating model principles

Aspirations	Constraints

• Provide an **end-to-end service** that is efficient and delivers a market-leading client experience.	• Organisational structure changes *will not*
	
	   – increase **layers of management**
	
	   – increase **overall costs.**

• Provide an **effective client-focused operations** organisation that is **accountable** and **transparent.**	• Open positions will first **consider internal applicants** before being generally advertised.
• Retain heritage and success in developing and launching new and **innovative market-leading products.**	• Decisions around roles and structure will **not affect staff eligibility** for promotions.
• Promote values of **client-centricity, transparency and accountability** for results.	

Define target operating model

To define the target operating model, explore options that best match the guiding principles. Each option should be based on a clear organising concept that is the basis for grouping activities and that together will form the overall end-to-end value chain. The model will usually be organised around one of five dominant concepts: (1) market segment (see figure 3.10); (2) product offering (see figure 3.11); (3) geographic location (see figure 3.12, overleaf); (4) functional activity (see figure 3.13, overleaf); and (5) process flow (see figure 3.14, p. 79). Each of these can serve as a starting point for defining the recommended changes to the structure of the company.

1. Market segment

- *Description:* groupings based on industries, market segments or customers

- *Advantages:* superior customer knowledge and services achieved through segment focus

- *Disadvantages:* duplicates activities, including inconsistent processes and systems.

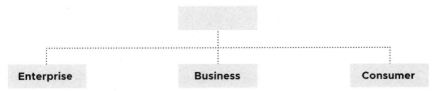

Figure 3.10: grouping activities by market segment

2. Product offering

- *Description:* groupings based on common product lines or business models

- *Advantages:* superior product knowledge and product line focus

- *Disadvantages:* challenging when customers buy from more than one group.

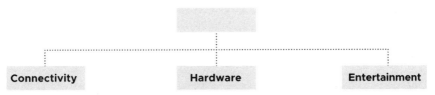

Figure 3.11: grouping activities by product offering

3. Geographic location

- *Description:* groupings based around physical locations (for example, regions or territories)

- *Advantages:* benefits of proximity to customers and sources of supply

- *Disadvantages:* can reduce economies of scale and standardisation.

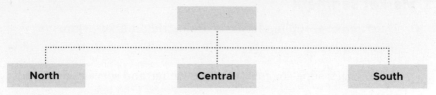

Figure 3.12: grouping activities by geographic location

4. Functional activity

- *Description:* groupings based on common activities or functions

- *Advantages:* enables deeper functional expertise and economies of scale

- *Disadvantages:* can result in challenging interfaces/hand-offs between groups.

Figure 3.13: grouping activities by functional activity

5. Process flow

- *Description:* groupings based on key steps or activities in the end-to-end workflow

- *Advantages:* superior customer knowledge and services through segment focus

- *Disadvantages:* duplicates activities, including inconsistent processes and systems.

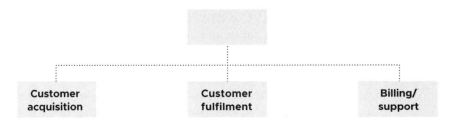

Figure 3.14: grouping activities by process flow

There is no ideal operating model to organise the company's functions; each has advantages and disadvantages. In reality, most organisations are structured as a hybrid of two or more organising concepts. Many successful companies will change structures as they adapt to internal and external changes. When deciding which structure to pursue, apply operating model options to the first two levels of the organisational structure, using design principles to evaluate alternatives. The best choice will be the operating model with the best potential match to the guiding principles.

Key questions include:

- What are the strengths and weaknesses of each operating model design?
- How well does each structure map onto the design principles?
- Can each of the design principles be measured and attributed to specific parts of the organisation?

The best organising concept will be the one that best meets the design principles, but there will be challenges and weaknesses in any model. These will need to be compensated for by other elements of the operating model design — for example, linking roles, dotted-line reporting, operating rhythm or governance.

Identify high-level gaps and status

Companies undertaking a transformation rarely have the right operating model elements in place to deliver the strategy. Design of the new model will need to ensure appropriate capabilities, capacity and culture exist in each part of the organisation to meet the company's strategic goals, particularly should strategic shifts be required. Sometimes entirely new capabilities and mindsets may be required if the company is to effectively compete and operate under the new strategy. Identifying gaps in the operating model will focus on assessing the changes or interventions necessary for effective delivery of the strategy. This can include both hard factors that can be formalised, such as structure, management appointments, defining roles and accountabilities, as well as soft factors, which can include ways of working and the company culture—styles of leadership, employee mindsets and behaviours.

Key questions to ask include:

- Do the company's capabilities align with the choices identified in the strategic plan?
- What shift in employee mindsets and behaviours are required for the company to succeed?
- What assets and resources will the company need to 'over-invest' in to ensure a successful transformation?

The answers to these questions should lead to a clear set of well-defined operating model interventions that should reduce the barriers to successful implementation. Common interventions can include: adding capacity and investing in key capabilities to support the strategy; reducing capacity and outsourcing non-core areas of capability; and instilling new ways of working that increase accountability, improve visibility of performance, and improve coordination and control.

Plan initiatives to close gaps to target state

Like any other strategic decision that forms part of the transformation, initiatives to implement changes to the operating model and the impact on the company cost structure will need to be planned and developed (see figure 3.15). Operating model changes should be planned in detail,

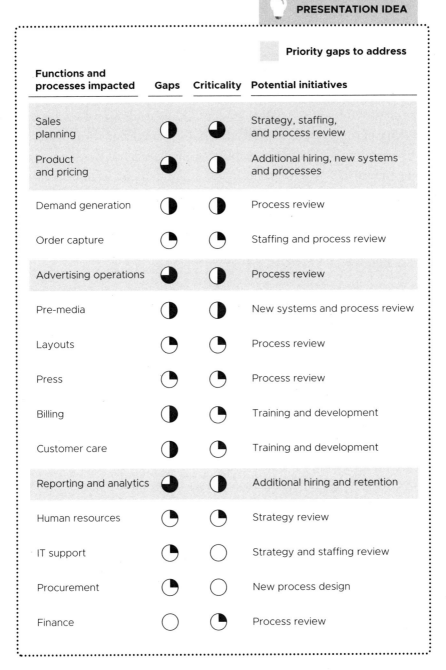

PRESENTATION IDEA

Priority gaps to address

Functions and processes impacted	Gaps	Criticality	Potential initiatives
Sales planning			Strategy, staffing, and process review
Product and pricing			Additional hiring, new systems and processes
Demand generation			Process review
Order capture			Staffing and process review
Advertising operations			Process review
Pre-media			New systems and process review
Layouts			Process review
Press			Process review
Billing			Training and development
Customer care			Training and development
Reporting and analytics			Additional hiring and retention
Human resources			Strategy review
IT support			Strategy and staffing review
Procurement			New process design
Finance			Process review

Figure 3.15: identifying gaps in the operating model

including organisational structure changes, and evaluating them from a financial perspective will determine end-state savings or cost target trajectories. The changes will be developed into an actionable plan with input from the company's HR function on how changes will be implemented. They can be either undertaken as a standalone activity or integrated into the company-wide transformation roadmap (see figure 3.9), with a defined initiative charter (see figure 3.7), depending on the scope and sensitivity of the initiatives involved. Financial implications of operating model initiatives should include capturing changes in full-time employees (FTEs) and salaries, restructuring costs, and the impact of any operating model–related efficiency initiatives (such as outsourcing or automation).

Consolidate financial impact

Changes to the operating model and plans for future initiatives will inevitably have implications for the company's cash flow and future earnings. This should be clearly understood and managed holistically across the company's financial accounts: income statement, balance sheet and cash flow statement. Each initiative may, on its own, drive a change to revenue, operating costs and capital requirements. Initiatives can also have one-off or ongoing costs and benefits. However, as a portfolio of initiatives, along with changes to the operating model, the aggregated impact of the transformation can dramatically reshape the economics and financial trajectory of the company. Consolidating the financial impact of separate initiatives and decisions into a single integrated economic model is therefore an essential activity for gauging the overall net benefit of the transformation and the construction of a financial pathway towards achieving the company's aspiration. This process also directly connects the initiatives to the financial plan, and company-wide KPIs and milestones that will need to be monitored. The completed model can serve several important purposes that include aggregating the projected multi-year impact of the transformation on the company's financial statements, determining incremental funding requirements, providing future budget guidance and deriving the measures of success for the transformation — for example, financial targets, KPIs and operating metrics.

Translating the overall impact of the transformation into a robust financial model linked to the company's financial statements can be time consuming, but the end result makes visible the financial impact of the decisions that will be implemented. A strong economic model for the transformation is not only useful for planning purposes, but can become an invaluable decision-support tool for a chief financial officer, financial controller or senior finance executive during the lifespan of the transformation. Even as transformation initiatives are executed and new information comes to light, the financial model can be updated and used to refine projections or make trade-offs, and evaluate the dynamic consequences of decisions. Building a comprehensive model that will allow the company to estimate potential outcomes will involve multiple steps: quantifying and consolidating initiatives; modelling the impact of the plan; producing forecast financial statements; and calculating net benefits. Key activities for building a robust financial model include:

- *Establishing a multi-year baseline.* Build a driver-based budget model (or reuse the forecast model from chapter 2 under 'Evaluate company impacts and base case'). This will split out the company's financials into key drivers and assumptions. The baseline should use current management expectations to drive future revenue and cost projections, reflecting the likely impact of external market forces.

- *Consolidation of financial impacts of plan.* Determine all the expected cash and asset inflows and outflows as a result of the transformation plan — for example, strategic initiatives, operating model changes and restructuring costs. These may include:
  - capital requirements to build or acquire capabilities and create capacity
  - capital released from efficiency, rightsizing, and sale or closure of non-core assets
  - changes to the company's capital structure that lead to a change in the cost of capital.

- *Model the impact of the plan.* Apply the impact of the transformation plan and each initiative to key drivers and assumptions in the driver-based budget model to produce multi-year forecasts. To maximise the impact of the plan, consider:

  - *Building the best case.* Frontload high-impact and easy initiatives to maximise net present value (NPV). Schedule activity to start as early as possible to accrue benefits and defer costs.

  - *Adjusting for constraints.* Make adjustments to the best case only if it is necessary to accommodate such constraints as capital, capacity, capabilities, risks, market opportunities, regulatory or legislative.

- *Rebuild financial statements.* Use multi-year forecasts to produce financial statements for the company (income statement, balance sheet and cash flow statement). This is sometimes referred to as building a 'three-sheet model' and outputs should include: changes to top-line, bottom-line, free cash flow, key KPIs and financial ratios.

- *Determine valuation impact.* Conduct a discounted cash flow (DCF) analysis to determine the NPV of the company based on the discounted sum of expected free cash flows generated by the transformation. (Note that the company's valuation is discounted back at the cost of capital, so improvements to capital structure can directly drive improvements in the company's NPV.)

- *Evaluate sensitivities of plan.* Conduct sensitivity analysis by identifying the value drivers and related assumptions that are least certain and have greatest impact on the financial results. These key assumptions are sometimes referred to as *critical success factors*, and the risks and uncertainties related to them should be explored, with mitigating actions put in place to reduce the likelihood and impact of adverse outcomes.

- *Develop alternative scenarios (as required).* Beyond sensitivity analysis, alternative scenarios can be developed to evaluate the impact that combinations of changes to financial model inputs and assumptions have on the company valuation. Different scenarios can lead to very different investment profiles and funding requirements. The development of different scenarios can be used to pressure test the financial plan and evaluate whether the transformed company will be able to succeed under a range of potential conditions.

Once complete, the transformation model should present the full financial profile of the transformed entity. The results can be used to compare the projections of the entity with the company base case (see chapter 2, under 'Evaluate company impacts and base case'). The difference between these two — the financials of the transformed entity and the base case — is the incremental benefit created by the transformation. Comparing the benefits of the transformed entity with the company's aspirations can help evaluate whether or not the expected results of the transformation will lead the company to achieve its three- to five-year financial aspirations (see figures 3.16 and 3.17, overleaf). If there is a gap between the aspirations and the consolidated financial impact, the top team can return to the drawing board to revisit the aspiration, strategic choices or initiatives and decide either to set more realistic targets or explore opportunities for closing the gap.

When evaluating the financials of the transformation, there are many different ways to cut and visualise the output of the model to understand the consolidated financial impact and what key changes to the business will be primarily responsible for driving improvements. Some common outputs that will be relevant to Board and top team conversations when evaluating the impact of the transformation include: forecast financial statements; revenue, cost and profitability forecasts for the entire program, or incrementally by initiative or theme; the investment profile of the transformation (NPV of the investment payback period, financial return, year-over-year cash required); funding requirements; waterfall charts showing how much individual initiatives or themes are contributing to future-state financial targets; and a decomposition of financial lines by key organising concepts relevant to the company, such as BUs, products, functions or geographies.

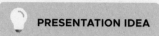

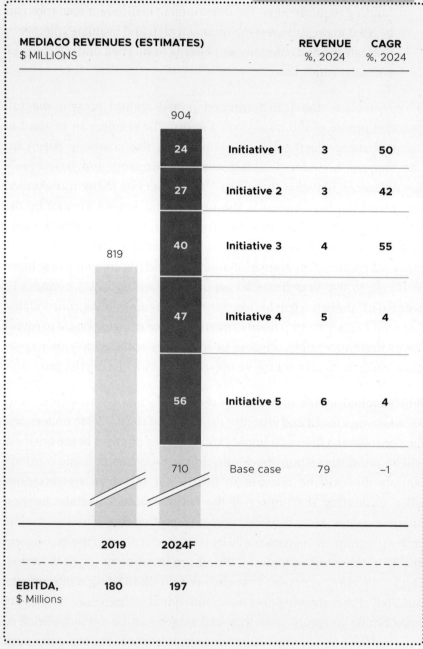

Figure 3.16: comparing company outlook to base case (1/2)

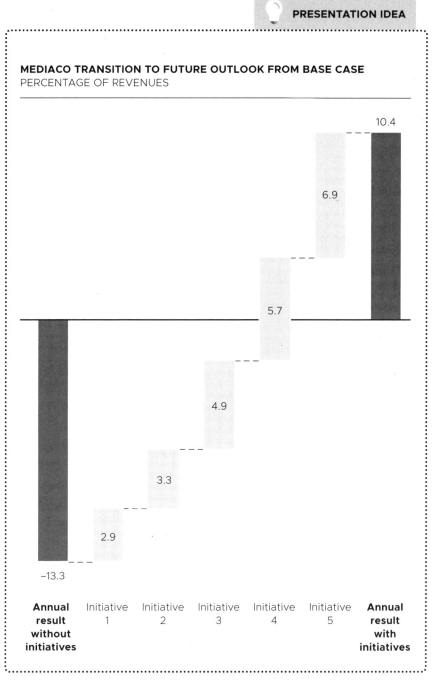

Funding will inevitably be a hot topic for any major transformation program and can become a major constraint. Sources can include operating budgets, retained earnings, different types of debt such as loans and convertible notes, and equity finance. The most suitable source of funding will depend on the financial health of the company and the relative cost of financing options. A healthy cash flow and balance sheet with low leverage and paid-down debts can be very advantageous for a company seeking to invest in the future, as it can enable access to a range of options, including the use of operating cash flows. For companies facing a profitability crisis or those managing cash and liquidity closely, operating cash flow may be inadequate, and there may be a need to secure additional funding such as debt financing or raising of capital, or releasing capital through the sale of non-core assets. When incremental funding is required, the availability and source of funding will need to be considered carefully, particularly if the company already has a highly leveraged balance sheet, or the cost of capital is high or access to additional capital is limited.

Boards and executives often consider a self-funding transformation to be the ideal scenario because it is perceived to be low-risk. For a transformation to be self-funding, the objective is to fund initiatives through incremental operating cash flow generated by short-term initiatives (see figure 3.18). The general approach is to pursue rapid revenue improvements through, for example, pricing increases and short-term cost reduction initiatives, such as operational, sourcing and procurement efficiencies. The benefits realised would be reinvested to fund new initiatives, thereby creating a virtuous funding cycle to sustain the transformation. In reality, though, some seed funding is usually needed to get early initiatives underway. It may not make sense to wait for the benefits of early initiatives to accrue when the company could more quickly set in motion existing attractive investment opportunities by drawing on other sources of available funding.

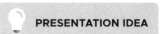

Initiative	2020/21		2021/22		2022/23		Total
	Capex	Opex	Capex	Opex	Capex	Opex	
1 Initiative 1	[x]	[x]	[x]	[x]	[x]	[x]	[x]
2 Initiative 2	[x]	[x]	[x]	[x]	[x]	[x]	[x]
3 Initiative 3	[x]	[x]	[x]	[x]	[x]	[x]	[x]
4 Initiative 4	[x]	[x]	[x]	[x]	[x]	[x]	[x]
5 Initiative 5	[x]	[x]	[x]	[x]	[x]	[x]	[x]
Total	[x]	[x]	[x]	[x]	[x]	[x]	[x]

Figure 3.18: incremental funding requirements by initiatives

Companies in mature industries whose core business is in decline are often faced with a deeper challenge to establish a self-funding transformation. This is because the margin compression created by declining demand or product obsolescence can dramatically limit the availability of operating profits as a source of funding. Meanwhile short-term levers may have already been expended as part of a management response to offset declines in profitability of the core business. When faced with this challenge, the traditional management approach is an organised decline, in which forecast declines in revenue/demand are matched by reductions in budget and headcount. Redeployment of budget and headcount savings should prioritise building capacity in viable parts of the core business — for example, markets, segments and products that can expect future demand increases. Remaining capital can then be reinvested in the company to capture opportunities for growth.

The financial model for the transformation can be used to establish performance targets for individual initiatives and consolidated performance targets that are to be tracked and monitored during execution. For example, PrivatBank, which was the case illustrated in figure 3.6, established a management dashboard which is used to directly connect the transformation plan to KPIs for monitoring by the Board (see figure 3.19, overleaf). This featured three years of operational metrics and targets linked to individual initiatives and aggregated to form company-wide targets that were to be met if PrivatBank is to realise its aspirations.

Generally, two types of measures are used to track achievement of initiatives: (1) activity based and (2) outcome based. Establishing a dashboard can draw management's attention to the success of individual initiatives and the vital key metrics (say, three to five) that directly connect the financial plan to the company's three- to five-year aspiration. Depending on the goals of the top team, these target metrics might relate to net profit, cost or income, return on equity or perhaps even market share. They are often conveyed as simple and memorable objectives — for example, doubling revenue, moving from top-ten player to number one or raising EBIT margins by 50 per cent. These financial targets can then be used as signposts or milestones to measure the company's progress towards achieving the company's goal during the transformational period. Depending on the CEO and Board's posture towards shareholder communications, some companies report transformation results to shareholders regularly.

Establishing both initiative and company-wide targets provides opportunities for the top team to set clear goals and objectives for teams and individuals against which KPIs can be set and measured. Usually the management dashboard is cascaded to staff from the CEO to at least three levels below. In recent years, Objectives and Key Results (OKRs) has become an increasingly popular management tool for setting and managing goals. The principle behind OKRs is to establish an *objective* linked to one or more *key results*, which can measure progress towards the achievement of an objective. Initiatives drive improvements in key results and both support and directly contribute to achieving the objective. The OKR framework can be used as a mechanism to cascade transformation goals and measures throughout the company. The OKR approach can also be used to ensure objectives are aligned both horizontally and vertically, with outcomes linked to incentive structures. This process can be repeated throughout the organisation to align the organisation and all employees to the results of the transformation.

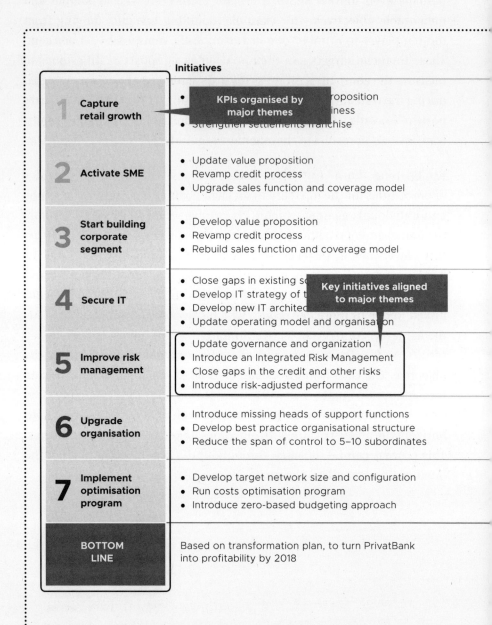

Initiatives

#	Theme	Initiatives
1	Capture retail growth	• ... roposition • ... iness • Strengthen settlements franchise
2	Activate SME	• Update value proposition • Revamp credit process • Upgrade sales function and coverage model
3	Start building corporate segment	• Develop value proposition • Revamp credit process • Rebuild sales function and coverage model
4	Secure IT	• Close gaps in existing s... • Develop IT strategy of t... • Develop new IT archite... • Update operating model and organisation
5	Improve risk management	• Update governance and organization • Introduce an Integrated Risk Management • Close gaps in the credit and other risks • Introduce risk-adjusted performance
6	Upgrade organisation	• Introduce missing heads of support functions • Develop best practice organisational structure • Reduce the span of control to 5–10 subordinates
7	Implement optimisation program	• Develop target network size and configuration • Run costs optimisation program • Introduce zero-based budgeting approach
	BOTTOM LINE	Based on transformation plan, to turn PrivatBank into profitability by 2018

Callout: KPIs organised by major themes

Callout: Key initiatives aligned to major themes

Figure 3.19: KPIs linked to initiatives for monitoring

Source: Based on information taken from 'Strategy of JSC CB "PRIVATBANK" until 2022"', page 32 'Direct connection of Operational Plan to KPIs for monitoring by the Board' https://en.privatbank.ua/about/strategy

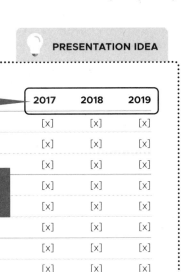

PRESENTATION IDEA

KPIs to monitor	2017	2018	2019
Lending volume, $Billion	[x]	[x]	[x]
NII (as % of liabilities), %	[x]	[x]	[x]
NCI, $Billion	[x]	[x]	[x]
Lending volume, $Billion	[x]	[x]	[x]
NII (over average cost of liabilities)	[x]	[x]	[x]
NCI, $Billion	[x]	[x]	[x]
Lending volume, $Billion	[x]	[x]	[x]
NII (over average cost of liabilities), %	[x]	[x]	[x]
NCI, $Billion	[x]	[x]	[x]
CoR	[x]	[x]	[x]
Capital	[x]	[x]	[x]
Share of NPL (excluding legacy, %) of lending	[x]	[x]	[x]
Number of branches, thousand			[x]
Number of FTEs, thousand			[x]
Total OPEX, $Billion	[x]	[x]	[x]
CIR, %	[x]	[x]	[x]
Net Income, $Billion	[x]	[x]	[x]
RoE, %	[x]	[x]	[x]

Callouts:
- **Three years of targets linked to financial statements**
- **Top three measures of success for each group of initiatives**
- **Achievement of milestones according to transformation roadmap**
- **Clearly defined milestones for activity-based initiatives**
- **Achievement of milestones according to transformation roadmap**
- **Overall impact of transformation on bottom-line measures of business performance**

Key features

INTERVIEW: ADAM WARDEN
SETTING TARGETS FOR THE TRANSFORMATION

Adam Warden is a global transformation executive and former Senior Partner at Bain & Company who has worked extensively with Boards and CEOs to drive strategy and execution in large, complex enterprises. During his career, Adam has led several company turnarounds and advised on many transformations, including those of Rolls-Royce, Ansett Airlines, Willis Towers Watson, AXA and, most recently, Fairfax Media. Adam's career has included balance sheet restructuring and acquisitions, strategy development and the execution of multi-year transformations that have enabled companies to achieve significantly stronger balance sheets, improved operating cash flows and margins, while contributing significant increases to shareholder value.

A common theme in the transformations Adam has led is the emphasis on being 'set up for success'. According to Adam, executive commitment and buy-in are essential. While the strategy is endorsed by the Board, it's the company's top executives who are expected to run the program, and it's the high-achievers three levels below the CEO who are typically selected to run the work streams. Another element to being set up for success is the importance of progress tracking mechanisms. By establishing a top-level scorecard, the overall progress of the transformation against the company's top-level goals and KPIs is made transparent so that employees, executives, CEO, Board and even shareholders can track whether the company is on track to achieve its aspirations.

Why are scorecards such a powerful tool when transforming a company?

When companies go through a corporate restructure or transformation, they generally have a scorecard. Strategy is one thing, but you then need to measure the results. So when companies are making big changes, scorecards are used to measure the impact. Scorecards also play an important role in project portfolio prioritisation and decision making. Deciding what to do, measuring outcomes and determining whether the program is on track — these need to be tied to the numbers; if they are not tied to the numbers, what are you tying it to? It's a recipe for disaster. So the scorecard gives the context for project prioritisation, to make sure the right projects are done, and to enable a dynamic approach to portfolio management. A good example of this is Rolls-Royce in the nineties. When they had a burning platform for change, portfolio management was used to reschedule, reshuffle and refocus the company on cash generation. A scorecard and value-tracking give you that framework.

What factors should companies consider when committing to a top-level scorecard and cascading through the organisation?

A CEO needs the backing of the Board before setting metrics. A top-down approach gives you the framework for the scorecard, while bottom-up gives you the detail and specificity that always need to be within the context of the strategy. A typical framework for developing a scorecard might have Vision, Targets, Key Results Areas (KRAs), and

(continued)

then operational Key Performance Indicators (KPIs). These elements would be linked together, so that KPIs cascade up, all the way to a strategic set of targets.

Developing the scorecard can involve months of hard work to link KPIs to the strategy and to make sure that there's no double counting. It's common on major transformation programs to set up business-case training, train the project sponsors and make sure measurement of results is embedded in the culture of the whole transformation team.

When it comes to reviewing and communicating results it's best to keep it simple. AXA had quarterly reviews, and measured their performance against targets. Whether dealing with analysts in the market or communicating inside the company, a dedicated communications team can play an important role in communicating the key metrics.

SUGGESTED **ACTIONS**

1. Define aspirations

Δ   Develop an aspiration for the organisation that defines a clear destination, involves and engages many people at all levels of the organisation, and connects with people on a personal level.

2. Explore strategic options

Δ   Explore strategic options that will enable the organisation to achieve its aspiration. Consider a range of options that reduce cost, deliver growth and build organisational capability.

3. Determine strategic priorities

Δ Prioritise or score a range of strategic options to identify the three to five strategic choices for the organisation to focus on.

4. Develop initiatives and roadmap

Δ Decompose each strategic choice into a set of initiatives and undertake high-level planning for initiatives to identify the scope, financial impact, milestones, timing and team.

Δ Develop and maintain a high-level roadmap that provides an integrated multi-year view of the sequence and timing of initiatives to implement the organisation's strategy.

5. Outline future operating model and organisation

Δ Identify the changes to the organisation's operating model that are required to overcome barriers or enable the organisation's transformation.

Δ Plan and implement operating model changes that will enable the organisation's transformation to succeed and integrate these activities into the transformation roadmap.

6. Consolidate financial impact

Δ Consolidate the financial impact of strategic choices, initiatives and changes to the organisation's operating model into a financial model, and forecast the future impact on the organisation's financial statements.

Δ Translate the financial impact of the organisation's transformation into performance measures that can be cascaded to individuals accountable for the transformation's success.

Further reading

Doerr, J. (2018). *Measure What Matters: OKRs: The Simple Idea that Drives 10x Growth*. Penguin.

Goold, M., and Campbell, A. (2002). 'Do You Have a Well-designed Organization?' *Harvard Business Review*.

Joyce, W., Nohria, N., and Roberson, B. (2004). *What Really Works: The 4+2 Formula for Sustained Business Success*. Harper Business.

Koller, T., Goedhart, M.H., Wessels, D., Copeland, T.E., and McKinsey and Company (2005). *Valuation: Measuring and Managing the Value of Companies* (6th edn). John Wiley & Sons.

Komori, S. (2015). *Innovating Out of Crisis: How Fujifilm Survived (and Thrived) as Its Core Business Was Vanishing*. Strong Bridge Press.

Lafley, A.G., and Martin, R.L. (2013). *Playing to Win: How Strategy Really Works*. Harvard Business Review Press.

Maasik, A. (2017). *Step by Step Guide to OKRs*. Amazon Digital Services.

McKeown, G. (2012). 'If I Read One More Platitude-Filled Mission Statement, I'll Scream.' *Harvard Business Review*.

Zook, C. (2010). *Profit from the Core: Growth Strategy in an Era of Turbulence* (updated edn). Harvard Business School Press.

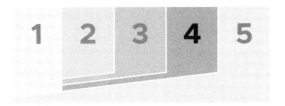

Mobilise

Once the way forward is established, the top team will need to shift their effort from preparing a comprehensive plan towards the setup of a broad-scale change and delivery program. Large, complex organisations, especially those with a rich history of success, are notoriously difficult to change. For any major transformation, mobilising the company and getting everyone to pull in the same direction — at every level of the organisation, including the top — can be a tremendous challenge. A commonly cited management statistic is that 70 per cent of organisational change initiatives fail. While this claim is not well supported by evidence, most executives are well aware of the challenges faced and the commitment needed.[8] Reasons frequently given for failure include a lack of sponsorship from management, resistance from employees and inadequate resources. These issues can prevent even the most robust and compelling transformation agenda from launching or cause a loss of momentum that leads to activity stalling. Successful implementation therefore relies on the top team putting in place both the capacity and the capability within the company to implement the necessary initiatives. To beat the odds and successfully deliver major change, top teams need to take full control of the transformation agenda, prepare the company for change by proactively building readiness with stakeholders, and also set up a stable execution platform for delivering results at scale. That is the focus of this chapter.

Preparing the company for change should start with identifying and prioritising stakeholders who will in some way be affected by the transformation, then assessing the barriers to change and proactively deploying targeted interventions. The focus of change management efforts should be the groups and individuals most important to the success of the transformation — typically those most impacted by the change and those with a high level of influence over the outcome. Once stakeholders and their importance have been clearly identified, it's crucial to begin to build readiness with these stakeholders and to understand the true sources of resistance and barriers to change within the organisation. Only once these issues are well understood can interventions be deployed. Preparing the company to change typically draws on three broad categories of actions: (1) communicating plans, (2) removing constraints and introducing enablers and (3) continuously reinforcing the agenda. Change management is most effective when interventions from each of these categories are deployed in a consistent and complementary way. Ideal actions to start with are practical and easy to implement, and deliver results that are visible to stakeholders.

To accelerate the pace, rhythm and coordination of delivery, the company should also invest in the setup of the program management infrastructure with the governance, support staff and tools to actively coordinate and manage implementation. This typically involves establishing the governance structure for making decisions and setting up a central team that can provide a dedicated focus to the management of the transformation — for example, transformation office (TO), program office or program management office (PMO). The central team is typically staffed with full-time program and project resources — for example, program and project managers, change managers, business analysts and other skilled professionals — who work alongside seconded line staff from within the company to support initiatives. The mandate of a central team can be limited (to, say, monitoring and supporting the overall program) or more extensive, with dedicated staff having hands-on involvement in the delivery of the transformation program, and being accountable for ensuring individual projects and work streams achieve planned results within expected timeframes and budgets (see chapter 1 under 'Mobilise a top team').

Lastly, mobilisation of the transformation program requires the appointment of business owners and initiative leads to provide on-the-ground leadership and to set up and manage individual initiatives in a coordinated and controlled way. The sense of ownership held by the top team needs to cascade to business owners and initiative leads, as their buy-in and commitment to the initiative objectives is critical for success. For each initiative, business owners and initiative leads need to be clearly identified at inception, since they are set the task of designing detailed solutions they will be responsible for delivering. This calls for a clear definition of the solution, detailed implementation plans with clearly defined accountabilities, and project budgets to be put in place. Business owners play a role in validating solutions and coordinating with the central team; initiative leads, on the other hand, define what activities are required to implement an initiative and take responsibility for the day-to-day execution to achieve the initiative objectives.

When building both the capability and the capacity to implement major initiatives and change within the company, there is often a clear case to establish the capability for change and delivery, such as a central team or TO, as a permanent part of the company's operating model. Faster cycles of disruption mean that change is no longer a one-off effort, so organisations should consider establishing the in-built capability to constantly adapt and renew to remain competitive. On the other hand, a TO is often best as a temporary structure, and by definition the transformation should have a start and an end. Whether the capability and capacity to transform the company is temporary for the lifespan of the transformation, or becomes a permanent part of the company's operating model, establishing the machinery for the transformation is a necessary part of the mobilisation stage, which, in the authors' experience and opinion, is a major factor in beating the odds and ensuring the transformation's success.

Create foundations for successful change

For almost any major change, commitment is tested before results are delivered, as overcoming stakeholder concerns and resistance is often a necessary step towards achieving success. Wilfried Krüger popularised the idea of the change management iceberg, which emphasises the importance of looking beyond issues of cost, quality and time. The concept explains that some of the most powerful barriers to change are stakeholder mindsets and behaviours that are often not readily observable and lie beneath the surface of the visible issues. Most people experience change as a journey, so individuals can be at different stages of adoption, with certain individuals much more open to adaptation than others.

Successful change management therefore relies on understanding the individual needs of stakeholders and designing a tailored set of relevant change management interventions. Executives overseeing the company's change should be asking: 'Does everyone from the CEO to the front line understand and believe in the case for change?', 'What are the barriers and enablers in our current operating system that need to be addressed for change to succeed?' and 'What actions will I personally undertake to reinforce the desired change?' In this context, the purpose of proactive change management is to build awareness and understanding among stakeholders, then to address individual capabilities and organisational barriers, and to sustain the change over time. In this way individual stakeholders move from being active or passive resisters towards being active supporters.

Many frameworks and theories of change management exist. A list of well-known examples includes the 'change curve' developed by

Kubler-Ross, the Prosci® ADKAR® (Awareness, Desire, Knowledge, Ability and Reinforcement) model, the Accelerating Implementation Methodology (AIM), General Electric's Change Acceleration Process (CAP), IBM's Change Diamond, the Influence Model and Kotter's eight-stage process. Many of these frameworks are commonly used to describe the phenomenon of change or provide textbook approaches to designing and implementing interventions to build support and overcome resistance. How they are tailored and implemented is central to their effectiveness. Seasoned executives will know that leading successful organisational change and overcoming resistance are easier said than done, and every executive will have their own mix of challenges to address when preparing a company for change. There is no silver bullet to winning stakeholders' hearts and minds, and generic approaches rarely provide an effective solution on their own. Preparing for large-scale change requires an understanding of the organisational context and stakeholder needs to ensure effective tailoring of change management efforts.

Facilitating change should start by identifying key stakeholders. These may be internal (such as employees, managers, executives and the Board) or external (such as customers, suppliers and shareholders). Certain individuals and groups will be more influential and important to the success of the transformation than others; these may be key opinion leaders, influencers, or key positions in the company, and they should be identified as central to the process. When managing the human aspects of change, it is important to understand that it can be an emotional process for stakeholders. The change curve is often visually communicated as a bath tub curve or j-curve. The journey can be broadly summarised as denial, resistance, exploration and commitment. The purpose of effective change management is to minimise how long the transition takes, and the impact of disruption during the process.

Developing an effective approach to managing change should draw on a clear understanding of existing levels of support from each stakeholder group and their specific needs. Assessing stakeholder readiness may involve leaders asking questions and really listening to responses, alongside formal interviews, focus groups and stakeholder surveys. Some form of assessment is recommended to identify and evaluate implementation barriers and where to focus efforts to overcome them, especially for larger programs with many stakeholders. In selecting the right interventions, conventional wisdom is that effective change management requires a composite of actions across multiple categories — including communicating plans, removing constraints and introducing enablers, and continuously reinforcing the agenda. These three areas broadly align to stages of the change curve and are consistent with common change frameworks including ADKAR®, Change Diamond and the Influence Model. When tailoring the application of each of these three areas it is recommended that change management efforts tilt towards key organisational barriers and issues identified in the assessment. Early in the process the focus is likely to be on communication but as the transformation progresses, the emphasis may shift towards breaking down areas of resistance and reinforcing the agenda to 'make change stick'. Nonetheless all three categories should be utilised. Each category of change intervention and its practical application will now be explored in greater detail.

Communicate plan and energise workforce

Proactive stakeholder communications are an effective way to shape opinions and drive a positive perception of the company's transformation agenda. Communicated effectively, a compelling transformation story can generate strong stakeholder support and promote awareness and a desire for change. This will usually involve the top team communicating the aspirations and major themes for the transformation in order to bridge the gap in understanding between top management and the front line. In this way the top team are declaring their intentions for the future of the company and presenting a clear way forward. While it's not necessary to have all the answers, the content of communications should be consistent and aligned with the company's overall transformation agenda. Communicating the transformation story typically aims to achieve several objectives:

- Present a clear way forward and create confidence in the future of the company.

- Align stakeholders with a common goal and purpose for the transformation.

- Manage and anticipate stakeholder objections by 'getting out in front of' stakeholder issues.

- Build a critical mass of support from a wide cross-section of the company.

In many large companies, the skills and capability to plan and manage communications may already exist in the form of, for example, internal communications teams, corporate affairs or investor relations teams. Dedicated communications staff who are part of a TO should work closely with these existing teams since they often have a good understanding of the company's corporate style and tone, and the channels for communicating to stakeholders. It is recommended that an integrated communications plan be developed and maintained for the duration of the transformation program in order to think through what needs to be communicated to which stakeholders, by whom, how and when. Preparation of a communications plan can be simple, but at a minimum should include the main messages, channels and timing of key milestones. A suggested approach to planning communications, message development and delivery of communications is outlined as follows:

1 *Stakeholder analysis.* Identify stakeholder groups and analyse their needs. Stakeholders may include investors, board members and members of the executive committee, employees and contractors. Stakeholder analysis should identify what is needed from each stakeholder, current levels of support and their needs from the transformation program. Groups can be broken down further into specific individuals or segments.

2   *Communications strategy.* Determine the communications
    approach for each stakeholder group to drive planning,
    scheduling and content creation. For the Board or executives the
    right approach may be initial one-to-one meetings followed by a
    group presentation, while for larger groups there may be a greater
    reliance on corporate communications and town-hall meetings.
    Common considerations in developing the communications
    strategy include:

    a   *Positioning.* How will the transformation be positioned
        given the strengths, weaknesses, opportunities and threats?
        Will the transformation be positioned as pursuing an
        opportunity (positive emotion) or addressing shortfalls
        (negative emotion)?

    b   *Substance.* What content will be communicated — for
        example, vision, strategy and plans, or a lower key business-
        as-usual communication? How much detail will be provided
        in communications, and how open will they be? Which
        aspects will be publicly available and which will remain
        inside the company?

    c   *Style and tone.* Are the communications represented as
        a personal communication from company leaders or key
        sponsors of the transformation, or reflect a corporate
        perspective — high energy and 'big bang' led by management
        vs low-key business-as-usual?

    d   *Distribution.* What channels will be used for distributing
        communications and will they be continuous or periodic?
        Will communications be centrally driven or cascaded down
        the line and locally tailored?

3   *Story development.* The narrative for the transformation program
    should be developed at different levels of detail for different
    audiences and purposes, yet remain aligned and consistent. One
    approach for planning messages is to build a 'message pyramid'
    that provides a framework for forcing clarity and structuring the

transformation narrative. Different levels of the pyramid provide increasing levels of detail and tailoring, but content at each level is consistent and vertically aligned:

a *Level 1 — Strategic narrative*. Develop headline messages and an elevator pitch that you can communicate within about 30 seconds and share widely. This becomes the primary message.

b *Level 2 — Supporting themes*. Cross-cutting themes or supporting details (such as 'why', 'who', 'what' and 'how') that are relevant to all stakeholders and audiences.

c *Level 3 — Tailored stakeholder messages*. Determine relevant stakeholder-specific themes and tailor details to meet the needs of groups and individuals.

4 *Schedule and plan messages*. Plan key messages by stakeholder and channel (new or existing, formal vs informal), with timelines and planned frequency, as messages will need to be communicated multiple times and in different ways. Communications are often cascaded through the levels of the organisation starting with the top team and first two levels, who need to own the plan, then the top 50–100 employees, then the top 200–300 employees — then reinforced regularly. Common ways to deliver messages include:

a *Roadshow / town halls / informational sessions*. Deliver a touring presentation on the transformation agenda and subsequent updates throughout the company, allowing for questions and two-way communication to create engagement.

b *Action workshops or leadership events*. Undertake workshops or events where participants are able to contribute to the transformation agenda or experience the issues and opportunities first-hand, as this allows people to experience the end-state in behavioural terms.

c *Internal communications*. Communicate the transformation agenda through regular staff newsletters or content shared through a dedicated area on the corporate intranet site.

5   *Develop message content.* Develop content based on the schedule and key message to be delivered. Messages should align with communications strategy in terms of positioning, substance, style and tone, and content should be consistent and aligned with the overall transformation story.

6   *Deliver communications.* Communications are executed according to the integrated communications plan. Communicators need high credibility with staff. When company leaders are delivering communications, tailoring messages will make them more authentic, compelling and inspirational — for example, they should deliver in their own style, role model changes and personally commit to actions.

7   *Incorporate learnings.* Once communications have been delivered a formal or informal mechanism for gathering feedback should be introduced to capture and incorporate it into the integrated communications plan. For example, employee surveys can measure communication effectiveness in terms of increased understanding and knowledge, and follow-up communications adapted accordingly.

Remove obstacles and create incentives

Stakeholders' support for the transformation and their commitment to change are not sufficient on their own. For change to succeed, employees whose day-to-day activities may fundamentally change as a result of transformation initiatives need to be enabled to act. Yet the nature of many mature and established businesses is that the current way of working is hardwired into their operating model, so even where employees want to change, they can't.

In large organisations where change is difficult, established structures, KPIs and targets, systems and processes, policies, rewards and consequences are all often oriented towards maintaining the status quo. If these aspects of the organisation are rigid, employees at all levels will always be pushed back into the old way of doing things. They may need to acquire new knowledge and develop the ability to perform differently. This may mean the transformation needs to deliver additional training or new experiences to help them think and behave in new ways so that transformation initiatives can be implemented.

Change management interventions need to target the sources of resistance and provide incentives to promote change. The scope of change efforts should address both organisational barriers and gaps in employee capabilities. Interventions may at times be cross-cutting enablers that support the capacity and capability for change across many initiatives; at other times specific change actions may be required in support of a specific initiative. In either case, consideration should be given to a select set of actions and their potential to unlock the status quo and drive change. Typical actions to remove barriers and create incentives to change include the following:

- *Organisational structure.* Group or link parts of the organisation differently to break down silos and align employees and teams in order to change objectives.

- *Resource allocation.* Reallocate operational expenditures within the company to build capability and increase capacity in areas vital to supporting the change agenda.

- *Management forums.* Add, remove or change the focus of key management meetings, including frequency of meetings, agenda and invitees, to shape organisational priorities.

- *KPIs, targets and performance management.* Set measurable benchmarks for change that cascade to each level of the organisation and hold people accountable for realising them.

- *IT systems.* Configure IT systems to support the desired change in process or workflow, or potentially introduce new systems or decommission old ones to support the change agenda.

- *Business processes.* Adapt existing business processes including what activities are performed, who performs them, and how.

- *Policies and procedures.* Terminate policies that block or inhibit change, or introduce new policies to promote or incentivise change.

- *Rewards and consequences.* Recognise and reward people for work that supports the change agenda and establish consequences for old behaviours (for example, changes to compensation and incentives systems).

- *Hiring and staffing.* Select and hire the right individuals for key positions, retain individuals who benefit the change mandate and, if necessary, replace individuals who are not suitable.

- *Training and development.* Train employees so they are familiar with essential concepts that support the change agenda and are ready to undertake new tasks, processes and ways of working.

Continuously promote and reinforce change

In recent years, concepts such as transformative leadership, Emotional Quotient (EQ) of leaders and 'centred leadership' have gained popularity among executives, who are more likely than their predecessors to lead major organisational change at various stages in their career. The common thread in these concepts is that leading change is not something that is easily delegated and that change starts with the self. Preparing stakeholders for change places significant emphasis on personal leadership and the ability to walk the talk. Stakeholders and employees are much more likely to embrace change when the top team and individuals with credibility are seen to lead by example.

Obtaining sponsorship from company leaders, influencers, opinion leaders and key stakeholders in the broader organisational ecosystem (for example, senior industry figures, major clients or union representatives) who can show visible support, personally enact change, empower others to act, and promote the agenda in their day-to-day interactions can all play a role in promoting and reinforcing the agenda. Executives with experience in leading major change will recognise that it takes time and proactive steps to get people dedicated to the cause of the transformation, but that actions that demonstrate a personal commitment will inspire, build trust and deliver returns well beyond the effort invested. To promote and reinforce the change agenda, a personal commitment to the change agenda can be demonstrated in several ways:

- *Show visible support.* Support the change agenda by participating, voicing support, and attending key events to communicate the transformation agenda and share progress updates by means of, for example, roadshows, town halls and workshops.

- *Personally enact change.* Actions always speak louder than words. Personal commitment to the transformation agenda can be demonstrated by spearheading changes to achieve transformation objectives and performing symbolic acts. For example, in a customer-focused transformation, executives may spend a day a month in frontline roles; in a cost-focused transformation, executives will visibly enact expense reductions.

- *Empower others to act.* Give people the authority and the necessary resources to succeed. For example, establish senior members of the team as change champions, and delegate responsibility for change to the line or operations.

- *Promote agenda.* Leaders need to enact the change by what they say and what they do, especially in their day-to-day interactions. For example, celebrate successful change and publicly acknowledge results, but penalise resistance or undermining acts.

INTERVIEW: VICE ADMIRAL TIM MCCLEMENT
MOBILISING THE ORGANISATION FOR CHANGE

In the early 2000s, the British Royal Navy (RN) faced continued pressure to become a leaner organisation with more efficient and effective operations. While the size of the RN's fleet had been reduced, its headquarters had not changed for over 10 years and its operations had become too large for the
(continued)

output required. Faced with a mandate to reduce costs, the RN Board established a major reform agenda to restructure the organisation and streamline its headquarters operations.

Vice Admiral Tim McClement, serving as Deputy Commander-in-Chief Fleet (2004–2006), was set the task of overseeing the RN's multi-year restructuring efforts while continuing to run the RN's day-to-day operations.[9] Under his command the RN instituted radical changes to integrate, delay and streamline HQ operations. The program delivered its targets in 21 months (against a 48-month target), which included staff reductions of 25 per cent (400 people) and £16 million per annum in cost savings, all with no measured impact on Fleet outputs.

A key factor in the program's success was the way in which Vice Admiral McClement selected the right people for key positions at the outset and involved staff at all levels of the organisation. One-star officers (two levels below Vice Admiral McClement) were delegated responsibility for designing the change program, including the structure of HQ operations, as they would ultimately be responsible for operating the new organisation once changes had been implemented. Additionally, a 'red team' reporting to the two-star officer responsible for the day-to-day running of the program was established at the outset to find holes, failures and missed parts, which ensured implementation was robust and anticipated constraints. The approach of involving line management to design the new organisation and being proactive about identifying issues and opportunities for improvement secured buy-in for change from the very beginning.

Why is it important to have the right foundations in place when leading an organisation through change?

It was absolutely vital as we moved towards establishing a new HQ that people understood what we were doing, why we were doing it, and how. At the start of the program the senior management team of both headquarters got into one room. I explained what needed to be done. They were used to accepting orders, so the purpose of the meeting was more about how we were going to do it ... We decided one-star officers would design the new organisation as they would run it in the future, while a two-star officer with the right skillset was handpicked to run the program on a day-to-day basis and mentor the team.

How do you build a broad base of support for change within an organisation?

It is important to be honest with your people on the journey by keeping them informed of what changes will happen when ... During the program, the RN Board received monthly situation reports and provided sponsorship throughout the program ... We engaged the Civil Service Union upfront, and throughout the program we got buy-in from our customers and suppliers by keeping them in the loop and listening to their ideas ... To gather new ideas from up-and-coming officers, we established a '30-something club' of the best and brightest who had been in the RN for about 10 years. We spent three days a week talking to people and listening.

What are the key elements for scaling and accelerating a major organisational transformation?

A program needs to be built on a rock-solid foundation, not quicksand. This means it can be better to move more slowly, but to get things right from the beginning. When building a team you need to have people who are honest. In particular, the people at the top need to have the moral courage to do the right thing. When you delegate authority, whoever is running the change program needs to have a real ownership stake. That's the most important point.

Establish governance structure

Establishing effective governance is central to the ongoing management and delivery of the transformation. In effect, the governance structure needs to create a joint partnership between the business and the transformation program. When the right governance structure is in place it enables decisions, risks and issues to be managed in a transparent, systematic and coordinated way at all levels of the company. Designing the structure for a transformation involves identifying the stakeholder groups that should participate in the management and delivery of the transformation, and defining how these groups should work together. This includes establishing the roles and responsibilities of each group, determining member composition, and designing the interaction routines that will be used to manage and oversee the delivery of the transformation roadmap. While the specific functions, linkages and naming of groups and roles that make up the governance structure will need to be tailored to suit the company and situation, a useful starting point will be to draw on the basic set of functions common to those in most companies:

- *SteerCo.* This cross-functional committee comprises the top team that oversees the delivery of the transformation, resource allocation, roadmap and goals. The SteerCo sets direction, makes critical decisions, and addresses cross-functional issues and roadblocks that can't be resolved by either the initiative team or the TO.

- *Core team (for example, the TO).* The central team that drives the transformation on behalf of the SteerCo is responsible for managing the delivery lifecycle for transformation initiatives, coordinating delivery and change, and solving problems and addressing bottlenecks during delivery (as discussed in the next section).

- *Executive sponsor.* This company executive and member of the executive team is responsible for the success of the initiative and has overall responsibility for ensuring the initiative objectives are met.

- *Business owner.* The business owner is the primary point of contact for the TO or core team for all initiatives that occur in their respective function. They coordinate with the executive sponsor, validate solutions and assist during solution design and delivery.

- *Initiative leads.* These team leaders oversee the solution design and execution of an initiative. They make recommendations on scope, milestones and deliverables for an initiative and manage the team and day-to-day delivery of the initiative.

- *Initiative team.* Each team member has responsibility for their own individual tasks and activities that contribute to the delivery of the initiative. As part of the team, members should work together collaboratively and communicate effectively to enable the initiative to progress effectively.

- *Change agents.* Change agents are often hand-picked frontline users or stakeholders who work closely with the initiative team and act as early adopters. They provide expert knowledge and support other frontline users in the adoption of changes.

Set up transformation office

Established for the purpose of driving the transformation program and initiatives on behalf of a SteerCo, a central team or TO plays a vital role in the successful delivery of the transformation. This team may be designated, for example, enterprise program management office (EPMO), program management office (PMO), program office, transformation office, strategic initiatives office (SIO), or coordination and delivery unit. While these names imply some differences in scope, focus and accountability, at their core each serves a similar purpose. The central team brings the capacity, skills and tools to track and manage initiatives along the project lifecycle and ensure consistent delivery of initiatives across the company. It can also play a vital role in coordinating stakeholders in order to dramatically accelerate the pace and rhythm of delivery. Further, the role of the central team can be expanded to provide targeted implementation support or to take hands-on responsibility for delivery of initiatives and the overall program.

The TO's mandate is usually articulated in terms of the transformation roadmap and objectives, and its success is anchored in delivery. However, it is important to define the depth of the TO's involvement, as this can range from providing light oversight and monitoring to coordination and facilitation to hands-on accountability for delivery. The latter option can improve delivery effectiveness but requires more resources and reduces the accountability of initiative owners. So the key questions in forming the mandate for the TO are 'How much responsibility will the TO have beyond support and monitoring?' and 'At what point does accountability for delivery shift from initiative owner to the TO?' For example, the TO may be responsible for the overall transformation program, each major theme and the 30+ initiatives, but whether this extends so far as to be accountable for managing thousands of milestones and potentially 10 000+ tasks is a critical design choice. The main areas of responsibility for a TO can be grouped into three broad areas:

1   *Managing the delivery lifecycle and reporting.* A standard project lifecycle (for example, concept, initiation, planning, execution and closeout) is introduced by means of templates, tools and standards that encourage a systematic, coordinated and repeatable approach to delivery. This is followed up with regular reporting to provide transparency of progress, signpost risks and highlight issues for management attention.

2   *Coordinating and facilitating initiative delivery and change.* Where initiative delivery requires a high degree of interaction between functions or can benefit from the centralised management of an activity such as change management or communications, the TO can become a single point of accountability for coordination to facilitate activity that will keep everyone on track to achieve their objectives.

3   *Solving problems and addressing bottlenecks.* To identify and address problems early, and to provide the capability and capacity

to fix problems, especially issues that span multiple functions, the TO can be staffed with delivery specialists. These specialists provide hands-on delivery support and work across functional boundaries. They can also be involved in preparing monthly/quarterly reports and work with business owners and initiative leads to ensure initiatives and targets are aligned.

Both program management and project management are mature disciplines with widely used, well-developed frameworks and practices. Approaches for setting up and delivering projects and programs effectively form part of PMBOK, PRINCE2 and agile delivery methodologies (for example, Scrum and SAFe). Peak industry bodies also train, educate and support companies and their members in project and program delivery. The Project Management Institute (PMI), for example, offers significant resources such as reference materials, tools and templates that can be used by a company's TO. The purpose of this chapter is therefore not to provide the depth and level of detail for delivery already offered by robust project management methods, but rather to highlight key considerations for leaders and executives in establishing a stable execution platform to drive results. Regardless of the preferred methodology, there are eight key processes that may need to be set up and operationalised within a typical TO to support the centralised delivery of the transformation program and initiatives. These processes are described in more detail here:

- *Project/Initiative onboarding.* Develop and review standard documentation for initiatives that can be used to facilitate planning, tracking and delivery (for example, initiative charters, initiative budgets and resourcing, and implementation plan). These are then incorporated into the transformation roadmap and overall program.

- *Interdependency management.* Identify crossovers between initiatives (for example, knowledge, outcome or resource interdependencies). Awareness of potential crossovers will be necessary to minimise delays caused through doubling up, resulting in reworking and solution conflict, and to facilitate knowledge transfer. Interdependencies can be captured in dependency matrices or included in a schedule.

- *Risk and issues management.* Programs need to maintain a process for managing risks and issues that will include continuously identifying, evaluating, mitigating, monitoring and controlling. A shared, centralised risk register can be set up and maintained for the duration of the transformation program.

- *Project change control.* An institutionalised process is needed for controlling and managing initiative scope changes. This typically involves a structured process for requesting, evaluating and approving changes to initiative scope. Major change requests should be reviewed and approved by the SteerCo.

- *Progress reporting.* Put in place the tools, processes and forums to systematically monitor program and project performance and track benefits using performance dashboards with KPIs and metrics.

- *Centralised communications.* Develop, maintain and execute an integrated communications plan (see under 'Communicate plan and energise workforce' earlier in this chapter) to keep relevant stakeholders informed and to coordinate communications from project and change managers.

- *Financial management.* To ensure initiatives are delivered within agreed budgets and to control program costs, the TO can centrally manage initiative resources, track budget expenditure, and manage payments to vendors, contractors and suppliers.

- *Project initiative support.* Oversee a small team (for example, a SWAT team) of suitably qualified delivery specialists to actively support the implementation team to solve problems and address bottlenecks. This function can be used to provide additional capacity to areas of need.

The planned staffing and roles in the TO should match the mandate and evolution of responsibility of the TO. The role of the TO typically evolves. To start with, they provide planning support in designing detailed solutions. Their role then expands to include coordination and facilitation, and lastly the TO provides additional project or initiative support with delivery specialists working on initiatives to help solve problems and address bottlenecks. During the mobilisation phase, the TO should be staffed with a program lead such as a program director and be part of the overall governance structure for the transformation. Other staff can be added as needed, or as the program progresses and they become essential to the ongoing progress.

Roles within the TO and central transformation team are typically filled by a mixture of contract professionals who can strengthen internal capability and internal staff who know the company, its culture and how to get things done. When hiring for the TO team, the process of selection should ensure that external applicants are experienced and well-qualified, while individuals selected from inside the company are top performers rather than simply an extra pair of hands. The actual roles in the TO will vary, depending on the scale and complexity of the program. Many large transformations may have multiple program directors, each with their respective portfolio of transformation initiatives to manage and deliver. Other staff may include project managers and coordinators, change managers and business analysts, or others with specialist or technical roles. Roles in the TO include:

- *Program director* — builds the program plan and execution strategy and is responsible for managing the program's delivery and oversees project managers to ensure the company achieves the overall goals of the transformation

- *Project managers (PMs) / project coordinators* — are responsible for one or many initiatives and their components, and will plan and execute work steps, monitor milestones/activities, and identify and mobilise the team to ensure initiatives are delivered on time and within budget and meet quality expectations

- *Delivery specialists* — provide problem-solving expertise to assist business owners or initiative leads as they address problems and bottlenecks; lead performance reviews and support preparation of monthly reports and SteerCo updates

- *TO analysts* — assist in the preparation of the performance baseline for initiatives, prepare performance reports and forecasts, and track transformation initiatives. TO analysts may also be responsible for actively tracking and managing initiative financials and performance for project managers and the consolidation of this information for the program director.

- *Change manager* — works with initiative owners and initiative leads and their stakeholders to prepare the organisation for change. Their responsibilities will involve gaining alignment, supporting the rollout initiatives and driving adoption.

SUGGESTED **ACTIONS**

1. Create foundations for successful change

Δ Regularly communicate the plan to energise stakeholders. This involves:

1. identifying stakeholder groups impacted by change

2. analysing stakeholder needs

3. determining the communications strategy, narrative, timing and channel

4. delivering communications to stakeholders

5. capturing feedback and incorporating learning.

Δ Remove obstacles and create incentives by selectively identifying and implementing management interventions in areas where it will have the greatest organisational impact.

Δ Continuously promote and reinforce change through personal leadership actions and empowering others to act.

2. Establish governance structure

Δ Design the governance structure to manage and oversee the delivery of the transformation initiatives and roadmap.

Δ Select and appoint roles in the transformation governance structure, communicate roles and responsibilities, and implement interaction routines.

3. Set up transformation office

Δ Establish the transformation office's mandate and determine the scope and depth of involvement in program and project delivery.

Δ Select and appoint key transformation office roles to centrally coordinate delivery (for example, program director, project managers, delivery specialists, analysts and change managers).

Further reading

Anderson, D., and Anderson, L.A. (2010). *The Change Leader's Roadmap: How to Navigate Your Organisation's Transformation* (2nd edn). Pfeiffer.

Kouzes, J.M., and Posner, B.Z. (2012). *The Leadership Challenge: How to Make Extraordinary Things Happen in Organizations* (5th edn). Jossey-Bass.

Agile Manifesto (2001). 'Principles behind the Agile Manifesto.' [online]

Murray, A., Bennett, N., and Bentley, C. (2009). *Managing Successful Projects with PRINCE2* (2009 edn manual). TSO.

(*continued*)

Project Management Institute (2004). *A Guide to the Project Management Body of Knowledge (PMBOK guide)*. Project Management Institute.

Shaffer, R.H., and Thomson, H.A. (1998). *Successful Change Begins with Results. Harvard Business Review on Change*. Harvard Business School Press.

Hughes, M. (2011). 'Do 70 Per Cent of All Organizational Change Initiatives Really Fail?' *Journal of Change Management* 11:4, 451–64, DOI: 10.1080/14697017.2011.630506.

Keller, S., and Price, C. (2011). *Beyond Performance: How Great Organizations Build Ultimate Competitive Advantage*. John Wiley & Sons.

Barsh, J., and Lavoie, J. (2014). *Centered Leadership: Leading with Purpose, Clarity, and Impact*. Crown Business.

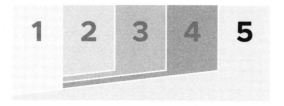

Execute and track

Realising the full impact of a company's transformation agenda requires that the top team sustain the delivery of initiatives and maintain a relentless focus on results. Executing the transformation as a portfolio of initiatives or integrated program with dedicated resources can accelerate delivery. However, the parallel execution of many initiatives at once, especially when significant scope, scale and interdependencies exist, is an enormous challenge for any top team. Major initiatives such as expanding into new markets, developing new products, technology rollouts and driving cultural change can be complex and require heavy investment and a multi-year timeframe to complete. When the stakes are high, company leaders should adopt a systematic and controlled approach with adequate governance and tracking mechanisms in place to provide visibility of results and to address underperformance. To provide an overview on how to stay the course, this concluding chapter is designed for top teams, executives and managers who are tasked with the challenge of managing and sustaining the delivery of a program or portfolio of initiatives over multiple years, so that major transformation initiatives are successfully delivered and the full benefits of the transformation are achieved.

To execute the transformation at scale, once the organisation is mobilised then everyone involved in the program, at every level of the company, has an active role to play in ensuring its success. Business owners, initiative leads and PMs need to provide strong implementation leadership by developing initiative solutions and translating these into executable plans and by staffing initiative teams with the right people, as well as proactively managing actions, issues and risks. To set up initiatives for success, PMs and initiative leads play key roles in developing a breakdown of deliverables, drawing up a realistic baseline schedule and preparing a budget for each initiative. This may seem like a necessary set of next steps, but the importance of creating a schedule and budgets for delivery is often overlooked as teams move straight from objectives and goals to activities. Building schedules to actively manage initiatives should include a list of milestones/activities at a granular level that enables day-to-day management, with clear start and end dates for items, and single-point owners with responsibility for delivery. Initiative leads then need to ensure that they have the right resources to lead, track and deliver the initiative or that resources can be secured to get them underway.

When overseeing the implementation of a portfolio of initiatives a stage-gate or toll-gate process is often used to validate initiatives as they move through various stages of a delivery lifecycle. The TO should ideally review initiatives, with the review and sign-off process being used to constructively challenge any activities or plans that seem unrealistic or are not aligned to the goals or objectives of the transformation. Initiative budgets and schedules are also sometimes held centrally by the TO or consolidated into a master schedule for the entire program. This creates consistency across initiative plans and enables the overall progress of the program to be tracked. A further benefit of a stage-gated process is that if plans are reviewed before sign-off by the SteerCo, TO, business owners and Finance, not only can any misalignment and potential execution gaps be identified before initiatives are begun, but that commitment to delivery from all stakeholders can be locked in.

As the delivery of initiatives progresses, managing their execution and that of the overall program relies on an effective delivery cycle and routines that operate continuously for the lifespan of the program. To drive progress, the program's steering, coordination and delivery need to work together in a virtuous cycle. An effective approach for managing delivery involves instituting a cascading series of regular meetings, with teams and leaders meeting regularly to discuss progress, monitor results and proactively manage issues. The results of these regular meetings, including progress reports, escalated issues and decisions, are then communicated up and down the chain. This delivery cycle is ongoing and for many programs is sustained over two to three years — a typical timeframe for the completion of major initiatives in many large companies. Small-scale tests and pilots are important for managing risk and uncertainty during delivery, especially if stakeholder readiness is low and benefits are untested. They will benefit from the support and oversight of the SteerCo and can prepare the ground for success before a program is rolled out. In this way, major initiatives will be delivered in increments with value proven along the way, promoting confidence and lowering the risk of under-delivery.

To deliver the overall goals of the transformation, the initiatives that collectively make up the transformation program need to be delivered on budget, on time and to the right quality. Also, financial and operational benefits at both an individual initiative and overall program level need to be tracked against targets. Based on the progress of the transformation at program level, it may be necessary to adapt the roadmap. It is not unusual for the initiative portfolio to evolve during delivery of the transformation as the strategy is refined, changes are made to the roadmap and initiatives, and forecasts are updated. Even with careful planning, not all initiatives in an ambitious program will achieve upfront targets, so the evolution of the program over time is inevitable. Lastly, as each initiative is completed it will be closed out, until eventually all are delivered and the objectives of the transformation program are met.

Set up initiatives and design detailed solutions

Once the TO has been set up and launched, the program director and PM can work directly with initiative leads and business owners to facilitate the design of detailed solutions for each initiative. Practical requirements to be put in place at the outset include: setting up logistics, kicking off communications, selecting and onboarding the team, refining initiative charters and developing the schedule. While project-based delivery of transformation initiatives is often the most suitable approach, not all of them need to be set up and executed as projects. The recommended approach can depend on whether the initiative is a one-off, short-term activity, or whether the initiative will deliver a permanent capability with repetitive tasks that become a cost, service or profit centre for the company. Different options for how to mobilise a team to establish an initiative can include the following:

- *Project.* The initiative is set up with a clear objective in mind, decomposed into milestones and tasks. It has a clear start and end and requires temporary resourcing.

- *Successive waves.* If the initiative has clear direction and the next steps are certain but the overall plan is unclear, taking a wave-based approach allows work to begin while planning for more changes continues.

- *Operational team (or function).* The initiative involves the mobilisation of a team to establish a capability that will undertake ongoing activity that becomes a sustainable part of the company.

Whichever option is used to set up the initiative — project, successive waves or mobilising an operational team — the process for designing the detailed solution is largely the same. Early interactions should be set up with the initiative lead, PM and team members to review and discuss the objective (for example, a kick-off meeting). The team can refer to the initial initiative charter as a reference or starting point for developing a detailed solution, as it outlines the proposed scope/

objectives, metrics and targets, and milestones, activities and team (see chapter 3 under 'Develop initiatives and roadmap'). Designing the solution can take the form of a project initiation document, business case or operational plan, depending on the context. It should include the identification of implementation options and any key decisions, risks or issues that are likely to affect implementation. The process of designing the solution allows for reassessment and should also be used to gain approval from Finance and the relevant business owner, and commitment from other BUs and teams involved in implementing the solution (for example, changes by the IT department). While this can seem like a lot of effort, the process of developing the solution enables the initiative team to consolidate all the information needed to hit the ground running. Relevant activities involved in designing the detailed solution can include:

- creating a work plan for developing the solution
- capturing the current state (for example, financials, operating metrics, roles, processes and systems)
- investigating implementation options
- developing the future-state design
- developing a detailed budget or financial plan for the initiative
- identifying how the benefits will be tracked and putting the processes in place
- determining interdependencies
- assessing changes to IT systems, or impacts to staff or positions
- identifying what the impact will be on the department's/ company's budget
- identifying the high-level milestones and activities necessary to deliver the initiative
- revising the one-page charter (see chapter 3 under 'Develop initiatives and roadmap') to reflect the detailed solution designed by the team.

Build delivery schedule and assign responsibility

Initiative schedules are the primary tool used for execution as well as tracking progress during delivery. Common examples of methods used include Gantt charts, Critical Path Method, Program Evaluation and Review Technique (PERT), as well as agile and Scrum, although in the case of the last two, managing the schedule is very different. Delivery can depend on the type of initiative, the preferred working style of the project manager and team, and expectations within the company and industry. For example, the engineering, procurement and construction sector often uses Gantt charts with standardised levels of scheduling for the delivery of large capital projects. These schedules have clearly defined roles and responsibilities and different levels of the schedule are used to manage the client, main contractors and subcontractors. On the other hand, many technology-driven companies prefer to use agile delivery methods, in which small, flat teams operate with fixed resources or timeframes, but work is planned flexibly and re-prioritised during delivery based on the needs of the user.

Many different tools and project and portfolio management (PPM) solutions can be used to set up and manage schedules. Many PPM solutions serve as one central work hub for decentralised project management with multiple users, which can be especially relevant to larger portfolios of projects with multiple levels of project management. The ability of scheduling tools to foster collaborations is especially important, because live schedules can be maintained without manual tracking and updates. Beyond scheduling, most PPM tools also offer further features that can be useful during delivery, such as the ability to track actions, issues and risks. A wide range of choices is available, and using a mobile whiteboard or wall space that allows teams to participate in planning the schedule and visually manage tasks is a very effective solution for smaller co-located teams. Among digitised options available, common solutions include the following:

- *Desktop software options.* Microsoft Office or Google Office tools can be used to develop and share schedules, and are commonly available and easy to use. Google's Office suite also allows users to edit simultaneously.

- *Purpose-built PM tools.* Simple online collaboration tools that provide basic schedule-management functionality include Tom's Planner, TeamGantt, Smartsheets, LiquidPlanner and Monday.com.

- *Enterprise solutions.* Specialised PPM solution vendors include Primavera, CA Clarity, Planview®, Planview LeanKit®, HP® PPM, Changepoint® and Microsoft® Project Server. These usually require configuration and end-user training but can meet the more sophisticated requirements of larger projects and programs.

When building the schedule, each solution must be translated into smaller groups of activities or tasks that can be managed easily in order to determine the proper sequence (including dependencies), and estimate the level of effort or duration required to complete each activity. Once a draft schedule is developed, it is recommended that PMs validate the schedule by conducting a walkthrough with the team, to communicate activities, create awareness of tasks and deadlines, and allocate work and assign responsibilities. Once the schedule has been validated it should incorporate all the essential elements needed to effectively coordinate and track delivery of the initiative, including: clearly defined activities/milestones and tasks, start dates, end dates and clear single-point owners. This enables the critical path to be developed, so that the dates of key milestones and the total duration/ effort involved in delivering the initiative can be forecast and used to measure the progress of delivery.

Schedules will often be decomposed into multiple levels of detail for different audiences and purposes. Usually, three levels of scheduling will provide the right level of detail to satisfy all audiences and enable effective planning—a macro, micro and daily view. Depending on the project delivery methodology used, there are different naming conventions and processes for managing the component parts of the schedule (see figure 5.1). For example, agile teams' work plans are translated into 'releases' and 'sprints' in which further detail takes the form of 'user stories' planned and estimated by team members during delivery. Regardless of whether teams adopt traditional project management approaches or agile, decomposing a solution should be done at a level granular enough that work can be assigned to individuals and progress can be monitored. The end result should then take the form of a simple task list, Gantt chart or Kanban board (see figures 5.2–5.3).

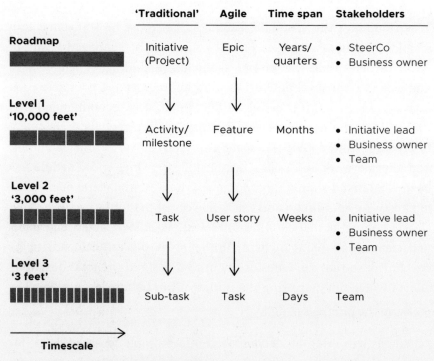

	'Traditional'	Agile	Time span	Stakeholders
Roadmap	Initiative (Project)	Epic	Years/ quarters	• SteerCo • Business owner
Level 1 '10,000 feet'	Activity/ milestone	Feature	Months	• Initiative lead • Business owner • Team
Level 2 '3,000 feet'	Task	User story	Weeks	• Initiative lead • Business owner • Team
Level 3 '3 feet'	Sub-task	Task	Days	Team

Timescale →

Figure 5.1: levels of scheduling

Activity/milestone	Responsible	Planned start date (DD.MM.YY)	Planned end date (DD.MM.YY)	Length
1.0 Implementation				
1.1 Setup of pilots	M. Kidd	::	::	::
1.2 IT integration	K. Tucker	::	::	::
1.3 Configure packages	K. Tucker	::	::	::
2.0 Training				
2.1 Tailor content by team	A. Espinoza	::	::	::
2.2 Train-the-trainer	A. Espinoza	::	::	::
2.3 End user sessions	A. Espinoza	::	::	::
3.0 Rollout				
3.1 Preparation	M. Kidd	::	::	::
3.2 Execution	M. Kidd	::	::	::
4.0 Evaluation				
4.1 Approval of pilots	S. Morley	::	::	::
4.2 Ongoing evaluation	S. Morley	::	::	::

Figure 5.2: example schedule

INITIATIVE BACKLOG	CURRENT BACKLOG	IMPLEMENTING		
		In progress	Validating	Done
Feature 7	Feature 1	(KT) Feature 3	(MK) Feature 5	Feature 4
Feature 22	Feature 11	(AE) Feature 10	Feature 17	Feature 6
Feature 7	Feature 2	(SM) Feature 21	Feature 16	Feature 7
Feature 22				Feature 7
Feature 7				

- Kanbans are commonly used by self-organising teams operating under agile principles and methods.
- Team members take a new item or task from the 'backlog' to 'in progress' when they are ready. Once completed tasks are moved to 'done'.
- The benefit of using a Kanban is that work can be visualised and is 'pulled' by the team, enabling continuous flow of activity.

Figure 5.3: sample Kanban board

Ensure resources to lead, deliver and track

Delivery of the transformation program can place increased demands on existing leaders and line staff and can require significant resource augmentation to execute initiatives. Organisational bandwidth is important because the line needs to lead the change and there are only so many initiatives that can be managed and delivered in parallel. Insufficient resources for delivery or a proliferation of initiatives can create bottlenecks that slow progress and cause delays during implementation. On the other hand, underutilised staff or over-resourced teams can increase costs unnecessarily and lower the rates of return on initiatives. The aim is to have the capacity to sustainably support the delivery of the transformation and make sure that all parts of the organisation are equally stretched. Key questions that need to be considered when assessing resource levels to support major initiatives include: 'Given the size of the task, are the right leaders in place?', 'What gaps exist in skills or capacity?' and 'Where are additional resources needed to deliver successfully?'

To deliver major initiatives successfully, there must be sufficient capacity and skills within the TO, initiative teams and the broader organisation involved in supporting the delivery. The work generated by the transformation program and initiatives should stretch the organisation's capacity to deliver, but not to the extent that they create unhealthy demands on the team or existing line staff. To meet the demand for resources, companies can balance program resource requirements with the capacity of the organisation. When individuals, teams or the company are overstretched it may be necessary to triage initiatives, loosen the roadmap — for example, defer initiatives, delay start date, pause inflight or extend timeline — or reduce the scope of initiatives so there will be fewer deliverables, features or requirements. To increase capacity, companies can invest in targeted training to enhance the capacity of line staff to support initiatives, onboard additional employees or temporary staff, or manage a tender process to appoint a supplier or delivery partner.

The main options to consider for sourcing increased delivery capacity include the following:

- *Internal employees — permanent, fixed-term or casual.* A company can completely control and direct activities, train a person in how the job is to be done and restrict the person from working for others.

- *Hired staff — contractors or freelancers.* A team of qualified professionals can be established at very short notice but they can be more expensive. Hired staff typically work more autonomously and require less management and oversight. They tend to be focused on outcomes and generally have less company loyalty.

- *Labour hire — such as employment agency staff.* Positions can be filled quickly and bring external knowledge and expertise. This is useful for meeting short-term needs if a company needs flexibility to end on short notice.

- *Managed services provider.* Management, infrastructure and staff are provided to support delivery, but this can take time to operationalise. Providers with offshore staff typically excel at transactional activity, using low-cost staff managed under service-level agreements (SLAs). Benefits include reduced capital costs, little or no hardware requirements and predictable monthly costs.

- *Consulting firm.* Services, scope or outcomes can be provided as agreed by arrangement. It can bring external knowledge and expertise, and is especially beneficial for meeting skill gaps. It is usually more costly to use consulting firms than using internal staff or hired staff, but they are scalable and can guarantee work quality and outcomes.

Conduct proof-of-concepts, prototypes and pilots

Reducing the initial scope or scale of an implementation by conducting a proof-of-concept, prototype or pilot is a common feature of many transformation programs. As companies face markets characterised by ever-greater uncertainty and volatility, being able to 'test and learn' when implementing a major initiative is important because it can improve delivery speed, increase flexibility and reduce risk. Wherever possible, programs should aim to deliver initiatives in small increments and with value all along the way. Taking small steps such as piloting initiatives with early adopters, customers or partners can be highly beneficial because this process can test the feasibility of the solution, generate additional buy-in and build the team's capacity. Once the initial scope/duration has been completed, initiative outcomes should be evaluated and used to determine whether expansion of the initiative should continue. Aspects of the implementation that went well should be carried forward as the initiative is expanded into new areas, while unsuccessful aspects should be stopped or modified in subsequent deployments.

When choosing between a proof-of-concept, prototype, pilot or full-scale initiative, it is useful to consider the initiative from two perspectives: (1) the company's readiness to implement, and (2) the potential implications or costs of failure (see figure 5.4, overleaf). As the company's readiness decreases and the cost of failure increases, the initial scope of the implementation should be pared back and the barriers to scaling addressed. Before deciding to launch a full-scale initiative, the relevant factors that may be useful to take into account include whether the solution has been clearly identified, whether buy-in from stakeholders is present, and whether adequate capacity exists to implement a full-scale program. Depending on the extent to which these factors are present, companies can choose from among several options for implementing initiatives at a reduced scale or scope to mitigate the risk of failure:

- *Proof-of-concept (PoC).* PoCs are small-scale tests with narrow scope designed to focus on specific assumptions that need to be validated, often before further investments can be made. PoCs are typically exploratory and not always successful, so teams should plan on integrating results into other potentially competing initiatives where PoC results can be applied.

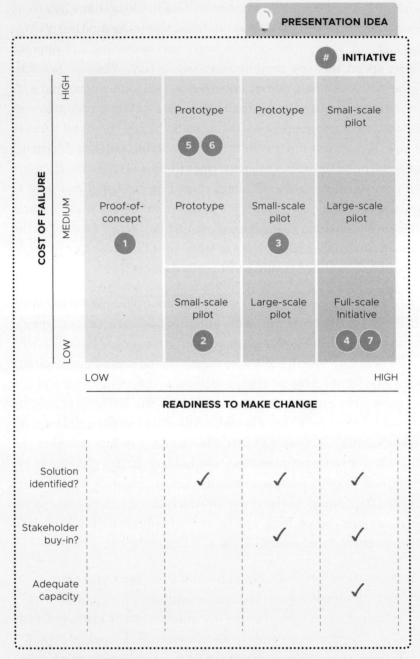

Figure 5.4: readiness and cost of failure determine scale of implementation

- *Prototype.* Prototypes involve end-to-end trials of a concept, product or business model to demonstrate the feasibility of a solution. While prototypes typically have limitations, they aim to demonstrate positive impact that can be used to gather further support from stakeholders and build experience that can be applied to improve the effectiveness of a solution.

- *Pilot.* Pilots are typically launched with early adopters for the purpose of building support and capacity. Where results are intended to be replicated, additional areas of scope for migration to the target state are grouped into logical waves for deployment. Feedback from the pilot is gathered and used to adjust deployment in order to improve the results of the broader rollout.

- *Full-scale initiative.* Delivering initiatives at scale is typically the fastest and most efficient way to deploy an initiative across a broad base, but the company's readiness for change must be high — with known solution, stakeholder buy-in and adequate capacity — and the risk of failure low, as both successes and failures are magnified when initiatives scale.

Manage initiative delivery

When effective management routines operate consistently throughout a program or portfolio of initiatives, delivery of the transformation can be managed quickly and confidently. By taking proactive steps to manage delivery, such as by monitoring progress and solving delivery problems early, initiatives can be adapted and course changes can be made so that missed deadlines, cost overruns and failures to deliver can be minimised. While many project-delivery methodologies such as agile Scrum or PMBOK prescribe their own routines and tools, the fundamental principles for managing delivery remain the same: teams and leaders should meet regularly to review performance, have in place mechanisms for monitoring progress, risk and accountability, and be able to deal with unexpected challenges as they occur until all initiative milestones/objectives have been met. This section describes how delivery can be managed over time by means of a simple hierarchy of regular review meetings, tracking progress and reports to monitor delivery, and by taking prompt action to address common delivery issues as they arise.

Maintain review cadence

Regular review meetings are an opportunity to evaluate the overall progress of initiatives and make course corrections during delivery. Most large companies will have multiple levels of management and many stakeholder groups involved in the delivery of the transformation program, so making sure different parts of the company work together effectively is often a challenge. One way to systematise the review process is to transpose the transformation program's governance structure into a hierarchy of meetings. Each group in the meeting hierarchy should meet periodically to review progress. Progress at each level will be reported up the chain, while feedback and decisions will be passed down. When operationalised effectively, all groups will be well informed; further, teams should easily be able to access management for support in dealing with risks, issues and opportunities and making important decisions.

When the agenda is designed, content, participants and frequency for each meeting in the hierarchy should be tailored to match the needs/responsibilities of the relevant stakeholder groups. For example, initiative teams might meet daily and use a dashboard or live scheduling tool or huddle around a Kanban to review progress. On the other hand, the SteerCo may meet only monthly, and meeting content may involve pre-work to develop a rolled-up view on initiative status with deep dives into key topics and recommendations. To make sure the SteerCo runs smoothly, the program director will first meet with individual stakeholders to understand any objections or issues. The results will be documented and made available to participants for pre-reading in advance of the full meeting. In addition to scheduled review meetings that focus on status updates, groups at any level may also choose to meet more often and for specific purposes as required by the needs of the transformation program. A group may need to solve a problem, reach a decision, provide status updates, develop ideas or build morale, for example.

For all types of review meetings, whether on the shop floor or in the boardroom, it's important that good meeting practices develop and that facilitators and leaders regularly assess their productivity and effectiveness. One way to enhance the effectiveness of meetings is to adopt a prescribed meeting format or set ground rules for review meetings. For example, many agile teams adopt a daily scrum format. The meeting is time-boxed to 15 minutes and the agenda is pre-set. On the other hand, PMs who follow traditional project-delivery methods may draw on the codified steps for running a meeting as defined in PMBOK, which includes having clear roles (leader, facilitator, note-taker), tight agenda, and circulation of minutes to both attendees and interested stakeholders. Other good advice for making sure meetings succeed includes meeting only when necessary, limiting the number of participants, distributing the agenda upfront, taking action notes and minutes, and reviewing these. Effective meetings are as much a leadership art as a science, and if review meetings are proving ineffective, delivery leaders and facilitators should take steps to improve them. This may mean following a more structured format, better inputs or pre-work, or improving meeting facilitation so objectives are achieved.

Track progress, risk and accountability

Tracking and reporting on the status of initiatives during delivery keeps stakeholders at all levels of the delivery organisation informed of progress, risks and issues. It is often advisable to establish tracking and reporting mechanisms early in the delivery cycle to ensure performance visibility and enable initiatives to be managed. From a financial perspective, this may require new cost centres or separate cost codes to be set up in the company's financial system, or tracking financials down to the general ledger. Progress reports can be used as input into regular review meetings so that timely actions and fact-based decisions can be taken to keep delivery on track. When deciding what is being tracked, how and by whom, it's this sense of purpose and utility that should ultimately guide efforts. As different stakeholder groups will have different needs, the type of information, the level of detail and the way information is presented will differ by audience:

- *Initiative leads and team.* At a team level, tracking initiatives may take the form of a regularly updated Kanban or schedule. Most online collaboration tools enable progress to be maintained in real time by team members and reviewed in weekly meetings so that actions and tasks can be clearly allocated, blockers raised and upcoming deadlines clearly communicated.[10]

- *Business owners.* For business owners, progress, risk and issues are often tracked through detailed initiative reports (see figure 5.5). When deciding format and reporting rhythm it's useful to assess and adapt existing reports, which should provide a realistic view of the initiative's status at a point in time. Common areas to include in reports are:

  - basic initiative details (initiative name, owner / project manager, date of report)

  - summary of project health (scope, budget, schedules)

  - overall summary of progress (actual progress vs planned progress, and next steps)

  - breakdown of key project milestones/tasks with progress and status

  - key risks and issues (new issues, open issues, key risks and how they are being mitigated).

- *Executive team.* For SteerCo meetings, status is typically reported at a portfolio level, which is provided alongside detailed initiative reports (see figure 5.6, overleaf). Rolled-up reporting of initiative status and dashboards prepared by the TO provide a portfolio-level view into progress, cost and benefits of the transformation, which can assist in overall portfolio management.

PRESENTATION IDEA

Initiative	Enhance retail value proposition	**Reporting**	
Business owner	Nicole G.	**period:**	w/e 27.11.20
Initiative lead	Jon N.	**Overall**	
Project manager	Paul P.	**status**	G^G

Initiative health

	% complete	status
Scope	30%	G^G
Budget	40%	A^A
Schedule	30%	G^G

Next steps

- Conduct needs analysis and develop insights based on survey data
- Showcase results and identify product implications
- Develop marketing brief

Overall summary

- Overall initiative remains on track with needs analysis and customer insights expected by 11 December
- Early initiative overspend (versus budget) expected to be recovered in marketing activity

Achieved since last report

- Customer survey response target achieved
- Product team briefed on product roadmap deliverable

Planned but not achieved

None

Deliverables/milestones	Start	Baseline end	Forecast/ actual end	%	RAG
Customer survey	12 Oct	27 Nov	25 Nov	100%	G^G
Research insights	27 Nov	4 Dec	1 Dec	15%	G^G
Product roadmap	30 Nov	11 Dec	11 Dec	0%	G^G
Marketing briefs	14 Dec	18 Dec	18 Dec	0%	NS
Campaign assets	18 Dec	15 Jan	15 Jan	0%	NS
Sales alignment	Mid-Jan	1 Feb	TBD	0%	NS

R/I	Key risks/issues	H, M, L	Mitigation description
Risk	Delays in regulatory approval	M	Engage Risk team early, keep informed
Issue	Sales capacity and alignment	L	Lock down team commitment in Dec

D/A	Key dependencies/action items
D	Regulatory approval of new products required before rollout can occur

Figure 5.5: example report format — detailed

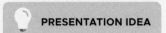

PRESENTATION IDEA

Status legend

G	On track
A	Some roadblocks (may require support)
R	Needs support to ensure delivery
NS	No support

Initiative	Lead	Status	Comments
Bank value prop	Jon N.	G^G	• All activities **on-track** or **ahead of schedule** • Wave 1 customer survey closed 20 Nov • Customer journey maps being validated
Revamp secured ending	Melinda S.	A^G	• Processes **requirements not consistent** across teams • Working Group established to look at standardised solution
Revamp credit process	Melinda S.	R^R	• **Technical challenges** in implementing solution has led to **significant delay** • Ongoing discussion to resolve; SteerCo review of solution underway
Enhance retail value proposition	Jon N.	G^G	• Wave 1 customer survey closed 20 Nov • **Analysis and segmentation** of customer survey data underway • Product team project onboarding complete
Upgrade sales function	Aarav M.	NS	• **Waiting** on completion of retail value proposition (dependency) • SteerCo review of solution underway
...	...	...	
...	...	...	
...	...	...	

Figure 5.6: example report format — detailed

When tracking and managing initiatives delivery, the basic requirement from a traditional project management perspective is that the scope, schedule and budget of each initiative have an established baseline before delivery starts (see earlier discussion under 'Set up initiatives and design detailed solutions'). During delivery, actual scope completed, timeframes and costs are compared to the baseline to show progress. Many PPM tools integrate planning, delivery and benefits realisation into one platform, so once the baseline is developed it can also be used to track progress and report benefits (see earlier discussion under 'Build delivery schedule and assign responsibility'). A centralised platform can increase speed and agility, and enable schedules to be updated regularly by PMs and team, while issues, risks and dependencies can all be maintained in real time to create a continuous view of delivery. If all transformation initiatives are tracked and managed centrally in a common system, this will have the added benefit of driving portfolio-level tracking and reporting, as many platforms support the roll-up of initiatives into a master schedule and development of custom dashboards to create overall transparency and provide stakeholders with a live view of progress and forecasts for both individual initiatives and the overall portfolio.

Troubleshoot delivery issues

Despite their best efforts to plan for success, top teams should expect unforeseen issues to emerge during delivery, and some issues will inevitably cause initiatives to run off track. When such issues are identified, leaders should rally the team to find a solution, remove barriers and continue to drive progress, rather than finding fault or assigning blame. Obstacles identified when solutions are designed can be planned for, or at least identified as risks, and monitored. In reality, however, many issues only become visible when they are first encountered during delivery; it's best to fix these often 'hidden flaws' in the plan early. The sooner obstacles are identified and acted on, the less resources will need to be expended to remove them. Ongoing reviews and the tracking of progress, risk and accountability (see previous section under 'Track progress, risk and accountability') are important routines for highlighting delivery issues early and enabling their prompt resolution. To get a lead indication of where obstacles might exist, PMs, initiative leads and business owners should use review meetings to actively probe and ask the right questions. Once obstacles are identified, how they are managed and the quality of the solution will make all the difference.

A common approach for identifying obstacles is to implement exceptions-based management reporting, in which reported results are compared to established rules and troubleshooting efforts are focused on those areas that fall outside the rule/benchmark. For example, an initiative that slips to 'red' one month may call for closer monitoring and attention while worsening status updates, such as two months of red status, may trigger the TO to review the initiative more closely and provide support. A trend of three reds may trigger a problem-solving workshop with stakeholders and call for the SteerCo to intervene. In each of these cases, it's the performance trend that determines whether corrective action or escalation is required. A red status on its own is not necessarily bad; in fact, dashboards that report a sea of green are generally an indication that teams are unwilling to report bad news and that greater transparency is needed, or that the overall program goals need to be more ambitious and pursued more aggressively.

Leaders and their teams should avoid or mitigate situations where initiatives are likely to head off track in order to prevent underperforming initiatives and avoid unnecessary stress and pressure. Of the many potential problems faced during delivery that can affect the success of initiatives, most can be traced back to one or several common causes:

- *Poorly managed expectations.* Setting overly ambitious targets, underestimating the true cost or effort required, or setting unrealistic timelines can lead to perceptions of poor performance and under-delivery. *Implication:* Set realistic expectations; anticipate problems to avoid surprises; and communicate progress regularly.

- *Lack of capability or capacity.* Delivering initiatives with too few people or a mismatch of skillsets can lead to poor-quality work, rework, low morale, bottlenecks and delays. *Implication:* Estimate resources carefully; build in sufficient contingency; and select staff carefully.

- *Unexpected scope/complexity.* When unexpected complexities emerge during delivery, teams often absorb increases in scope that place additional pressure on budgets and timelines. *Implication:* Have sufficient contingency to accommodate unforeseen complexity; formalise increases in scope as changes to the plan and raise as key decisions.

- *Lack of accountability.* When initiatives lack clearly defined roles, responsibilities and deliverables, people can avoid tasks and shift blame. *Implication:* Clearly define deliverables, roles and responsibilities, and establish clear owners and accountability; hold people accountable.

- *Conflicts and miscommunications.* Conflicts and miscommunications among team members, leaders and stakeholders, especially when the stakes are high, can become a significant barrier to progress. *Implication:* Ensure proper communication flow at every level; promote collaboration and team work.

- *Unmet interdependencies.* Not all aspects of an initiative are necessarily under the full control of the delivery team. Sometimes delivery relies on external factors outside the team's control, which may lead to delays. *Implication:* Ensure alignment and communication with interdependent activities; monitor interdependencies and maintain contingency plans.

The issues faced by teams during delivery are usually simple problems that have common-sense solutions. Managers or TO staff will usually recognise these issues and take practical steps to remedy them. For example, if a person who is accountable is not delivering, the manager should make sure the task is clearly understood and that the person is capable of delivering the task, and should establish clear consequences if the task is not delivered. But issues may fall into a second category — that of obstacles with no obvious solutions. It's these issues that normally require additional support from the TO to assess the situation, diagnose and plan, identify solutions, and develop recommendations or an implementation plan. Problem-solving workshops may be needed. There is also a third category of issues: those with high criticality and the potential for significant impact on the success of the program. These warrant close leadership attention. They tend to be larger and more complex to solve, often requiring SteerCo involvement to manage difficult trade-offs, make adjustments to plans, or perhaps change goals and objectives.

INTERVIEW: MICHAEL WELCH
SUSTAINING A MULTI-YEAR PROGRAM

Michael Welch is an accomplished delivery executive who has operated large-scale, complex, multi-year transformation programs at AGL Energy, News Corp and NBN Co. Michael shares some practical insights on his approach to driving and delivering results at scale in these large organisations and helping executive teams to embed and sustain large transformation programs.

How do you keep a transformation program on track during delivery?

It's important to give teams a degree of autonomy in how they work by focusing on the outcome of the components being delivered, rather than how it is achieved. This creates a stronger sense of ownership, and so long as these outcomes contribute to the overall purpose, and are aligned with the principles of the transformation, more issues can and will be resolved at a team level.

A good cadence of meetings, starting with daily stand-ups within each working group and clear escalation paths, can help keep the program on track. This gives leaders at all levels visibility on the program's progress and any issues that arise, and enables tough decisions and trade-offs that keep the program on track.

What role should a transformation office or program office play during delivery?

A project office can provide teams with invaluable support, which can include playing a role in coordinating activity, reporting and providing tools and methods that working groups can use. In some cases, project offices might make use of specialised software and at other times desktop applications such as Excel within a structured framework will do the job.

Close out initiatives

When initiatives have been delivered, even though the team may be ready to declare victory, it is good practice to have a formal process to close out initiatives and capture learnings. The steps to closing out an initiative should be tailored to the type of initiative and the stakeholders involved; requirements and level of formality normally increase with the scale, value and risk of the initiative/project. For example, major initiatives involving multiple vendors and complex commercials, such as large capital projects, are likely to follow a formal closeout process with relevant activities built into the schedule. For major initiatives like these, there are advantages to conducting a rigorous closeout for the team, company and providers. Close out activities are used to validate delivery, secure stakeholder sign-off and celebrate completion. They can make the success of the initiative visible and mitigate commercial risks. At the other end of the spectrum, the closeout of smaller initiatives completed mainly by internal staff can be more informal, with a focus on tying off loose ends and celebrating success, and recognising the individuals and team involved.

Most project delivery approaches will have closeout steps built into the project management lifecycle. Generally, these will include the following:

- *Confirming initiative delivery.* The PM validates the initiative's delivery. This is often based on comparing actual results or completed activities to clearly defined acceptance criteria agreed before the initiative was started — the Initiative Charter. The acceptance criteria will depend on how success was defined at the outset:

  - Activity-based measures confirm that all activities/tasks have been completed (for example, user requirements captured, IT system configured, testing complete).

  - Outcome-based measures confirm that targets have been achieved (for example, net income targets, cost-reduction targets, customer-satisfaction score).

- *Obtain stakeholder agreement/sign-off.* Sign-off from the executive sponsor confirms that the initiative has been delivered. This is often based on clearly defined acceptance criteria agreed before the initiative was started (Initiative Charter). Any gaps should be identified and form part of a punch list outlining what is left to be done before the initiative can be officially signed off.

- *Transition ongoing activities to line.* Any ongoing activity that must continue beyond the life of the initiative needs to be transferred to line staff. Initiatives should aim for a smooth hand-off from initiative team to operations. Typically, this involves a period when the initiative team and line staff will work together until the team gradually steps back and activities move into operations.

- *Closing initiative activities.* Any activities relevant only for the period during which the initiative is being delivered need to be closed. Teams must:

  - *release resources* — making reasonable efforts to transition team members to new projects or end contracts

  - *close finances* — closing the books to establish final balance and prevent further costs from being booked to the initiative

  - *close and archive documentation* — consolidating all project documents and transferring them to the initiative's executive sponsor or their delegate

  - *close location* — clearing physical locations and terminating building and system access used by the delivery team (as required).

- *Document lessons learned.* Knowledge and experience developed by the team over the course of the initiative can often be incorporated into future initiatives — for example, identifying horizontal deployment opportunities or actions to incorporate into future projects. A post-implementation review (PIR), especially for major projects and investments, can be an opportunity to critically evaluate results and whether initiatives achieve their intended outcomes. Areas to look at include the following:

  - Was budget met? (spend vs actuals)

  - Were all milestones met?

  - Was original scope delivered? If not, what were the reasons?

  - Did project meet expected outcomes and KPIs?

  - How did the costs compare with the benefits? (cost vs benefits)

  - Were savings fully realised?

  - Was the sponsor satisfied?

  - Were lessons learned on how to avoid issues in the future?

- *Team recognition*. Delivery of a major initiative is a great achievement and it's important to recognise the efforts of the team and individuals involved — both privately and in public.

  - Privately rewarding and recognising individuals who contributed significantly can play a major role in motivating and retaining high performers.

  - Publicly celebrating results builds commitment and can be used to reinforce the importance of transformation. It can also be important in sustaining a multi-year journey and overcoming fatigue.

Evaluate impact of transformation against targets

During the company's transformational period, there can be many positive signals that a change is taking hold. This may include a visible shift in the company's financials, reports of progress in key initiatives, and positive commentary in the press and financial markets. The real measure of success, however, is the progress the company has made in fulfilling its aspirations. The 'management dashboard' established when the targets for the transformation were originally set provides a solid basis for evaluating progress per initiative and the aggregated results. The dashboard will enable actual results to be compared to quarterly or annual targets, which roll up to the central measures of company performance (including top line, bottom line and return on equity). Typically, measures of success relevant to the Board or top management can be reduced to three to five metrics that matter. Figure 5.7 offers an example of how individual initiatives and overall company results for the transformation are tracked and reported against targets. Useful elements to include in the management dashboard are whether financial and operational targets, KPIs and activity milestones are being met, the percentage variance to target and the performance trend over preceding periods.

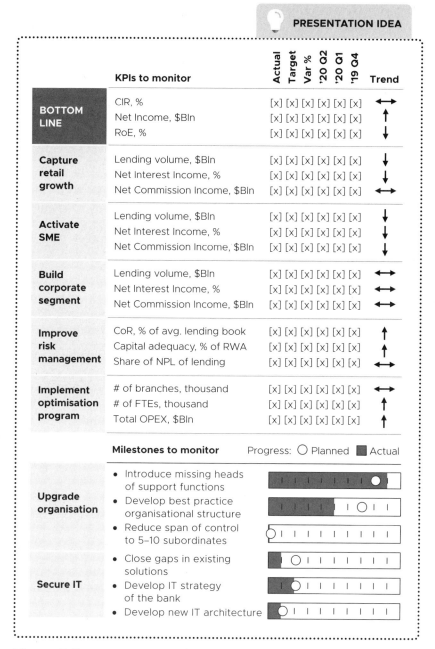

KPIs to monitor	Actual	Target	Var %	'20 Q2	'20 Q1	'19 Q4	Trend
BOTTOM LINE							
CIR, %	[x]	[x]	[x]	[x]	[x]	[x]	↔
Net Income, $Bln	[x]	[x]	[x]	[x]	[x]	[x]	↑
RoE, %	[x]	[x]	[x]	[x]	[x]	[x]	↓
Capture retail growth							
Lending volume, $Bln	[x]	[x]	[x]	[x]	[x]	[x]	↓
Net Interest Income, %	[x]	[x]	[x]	[x]	[x]	[x]	↓
Net Commission Income, $Bln	[x]	[x]	[x]	[x]	[x]	[x]	↔
Activate SME							
Lending volume, $Bln	[x]	[x]	[x]	[x]	[x]	[x]	↓
Net Interest Income, %	[x]	[x]	[x]	[x]	[x]	[x]	↓
Net Commission Income, $Bln	[x]	[x]	[x]	[x]	[x]	[x]	↓
Build corporate segment							
Lending volume, $Bln	[x]	[x]	[x]	[x]	[x]	[x]	↔
Net Interest Income, %	[x]	[x]	[x]	[x]	[x]	[x]	↔
Net Commission Income, $Bln	[x]	[x]	[x]	[x]	[x]	[x]	↔
Improve risk management							
CoR, % of avg. lending book	[x]	[x]	[x]	[x]	[x]	[x]	↑
Capital adequacy, % of RWA	[x]	[x]	[x]	[x]	[x]	[x]	↑
Share of NPL of lending	[x]	[x]	[x]	[x]	[x]	[x]	↔
Implement optimisation program							
# of branches, thousand	[x]	[x]	[x]	[x]	[x]	[x]	↔
# of FTEs, thousand	[x]	[x]	[x]	[x]	[x]	[x]	↑
Total OPEX, $Bln	[x]	[x]	[x]	[x]	[x]	[x]	↑

Milestones to monitor   Progress: ○ Planned ■ Actual

Upgrade organisation
- Introduce missing heads of support functions
- Develop best practice organisational structure
- Reduce span of control to 5–10 subordinates

Secure IT
- Close gaps in existing solutions
- Develop IT strategy of the bank
- Develop new IT architecture

Figure 5.7: management dashboard to measure success

Source: Fictional adaptation of KPIs and metrics for 'PrivatBank 2022 Strategy' into a management dashboard.

Delivery of the transformation program can span several years, as often a sustained effort is required to meet ambitious targets. During periods of significant industry and market disruption, both the internal and external situation can change dramatically, and this can require the top team to evaluate progress periodically and make course corrections. By proceeding adaptively, top teams can act to take full advantage of new opportunities as they emerge, or to navigate difficult or unexpected challenges one step at a time. This ability to constantly adapt remains an essential advantage for competing in the digital age. With this in mind, adapting to change during the company's transformation journey is a constant requirement and top teams should respond to this by ensuring the transformation evolves as new information becomes available. This includes:

- regularly updating forecasts based on more accurate assumptions and new information to maintain an accurate long-term view

- refining the strategy, roadmap and initiatives based on the most up-to-date information about the industry, market or competitors

- reprioritising initiatives based on actual results — for example, building on areas delivering greater-than-expected results, and deferring lower value initiatives that are not time-bound.

SUGGESTED **ACTIONS**

1. Set up initiatives and design detailed solutions

Δ   Transformation office and business owners to work together to set up logistics, develop kick-off communications and onboard initiative teams to develop detailed solutions for each initiative.

2. Build delivery schedule and assign responsibility

Δ   Translate solutions for initiatives into smaller groups of activities or tasks that can be planned and assigned to individual owners with clear accountability.

Δ Transformation office may choose to oversee the capture of delivery schedules into a central project or portfolio management solution.

3. Ensure resources to lead, deliver and track

Δ Identify resource gaps and augment the organisation with the skills and capacity required (e.g. new employees, hiring contractors, engaging labour hire organisations, outsourcing activities to managed service providers or engaging consulting firms).

4. Conduct proof-of-concepts, prototypes and pilots

Δ Assess and adapt the scope and scale of initiative rollouts as needed to address the cost of failure and readiness of the organisation to change.

5. Manage initiative delivery

Δ Establish and sustain delivery routines to drive ongoing progress, including:

- maintaining a hierarchy of regular meetings to evaluate progress and make course corrections

- ongoing tracking and reporting of initiative and program status to ensure visibility of progress, risks and issues

- proactively identifying and troubleshooting delivery issues.

6. Close out initiatives

Δ Implement formal closeout procedures for initiatives once they have been delivered to validate delivery, secure sign-off and celebrate completion.

(continued)

7. Evaluate impact of the transformation against targets

Δ   Periodically track and review overall KPIs and milestones for the transformation to evaluate progress against targets.

Δ   Incorporate lessons learned and results into future activities, including:

- updating forecasts

- refining strategy, roadmap and initiatives

- reprioritising initiatives based on results.

Further reading

Agile Manifesto (2001). 'Principles behind the Agile Manifesto.' [online]

Melton, T., and Iles-Smith, P. (2009). *Managing Project Delivery: Maintaining Control and Achieving Success*. Butterworth-Heinemann.

Murray, A., Bennett, N., and Bentley, C. (2009). *Managing successful projects with PRINCE2* (2009 edn manual). TSO.

Project Management Institute (2004). *A Guide to the Project Management Body of Knowledge (PMBOK guide)*. Project Management Institute.

APPENDIX I: DIAGNOSING COMPANY PERFORMANCE

A step-by-step approach to diagnosing company performance is outlined in figure AI.1. Further details describing each step follow.

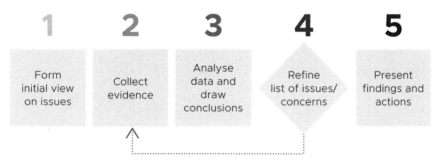

Figure AI.1: a structured approach to diagnosing company performance

1. Form initial view on issues

Start by identifying what needs to be done. Prepare a list of assumed issues based on an initial understanding of management concerns and the broader issues facing the company and industry. The list also identifies what needs to be changed and should focus on the key levers in the business to identify what drives revenue, costs and savings, and which levers have the greatest impact on performance. A P&L structure or a value driver tree guides a comprehensive and structured approach to identifying issues, and helps make sure the issues identified are complete (no gaps), distinct (not overlapping) and consistent (same level of detail). For example, figure AI.2 shows how a value-driver tree has been used to systematically review each of the drivers of shareholder value and consider the potential issues in each. Each assumed issue then forms the basis of the diagnostic scope and plan (see figure AI.3, overleaf).

2. Collect evidence

Combining data requests to Finance with information gathered from initial interviews with key executives forms the basis of company input. Ideally, the relevant measurement period should ensure five years of historic data, current year-to-date actuals and budget, and three years of forecasts, but industries with longer operating cycles may require a longer time series. All the key information collected should be clearly linked to the issues identified (see figure AI.2), and typically includes:

- financial statements, including
    - P&L (consolidated and by department)
    - balance sheet
    - cash flow statement
- revenue breakdown, including
    - sales by product line
    - price changes over time
- cost breakdowns, including
    - capital expenditure by project or activity
    - fixed costs
    - variable costs

Shareholder value		
Revenue growth	**Volume**	Unit sales in core segments and product lines continues to decline, while customer take up of software subscriptions has been slower than expected with high churn and not able to dramatically offset rate of decline
	Price	Average invoice prices are declining in core product lines due to competitive discounting and aggressive promotions
Operating margin	**COGS**	Fixed costs have remained flat over time Overall manufacturing costs have increased due to: • weaker local dollar on internationally sourced components • rise in unit assembly costs due to expanded offering of customisable products which are more labour intensive to assemble
	Sales and marketing	Sales and marketing costs remain high due to high cost of online marketing despite significant reductions in sales staff
	General and administrative	Realisation of cost efficiencies in general overheads has been slower than budgeted despite substantial layoff of warehouse staff
	Research and development	Major R&D project spend and commitments have decreased along with reduction in R&D headcount
	Income tax	Income tax rate has increased as a proportion of sales due to fewer R&D offsets
Asset efficiency	**Property, plant and equipment**	Warehouse closures and consolidation across national network have reduced overall asset footprint of the company
	Inventory	Stock holdings have increased due to proliferation of components required in the unit assembly process
	Receivables and payables	Loosening of existing payment terms to large distributors is resulting in increased receivables and days outstanding

Figure AI.2: value-driver tree and initial issues

DIAGNOSTIC WORK PLAN

Assumed issues	Analysis	Data required	Responsible	Deadline	Actual answer	Degree of concern
Unit sales in core product lines is declining at a rapid pace	Chart showing sales revenue by product line (y-axis) over last 3 years (x-axis)	product sales data	Daniel P.	17 July	True/ False	...
Customer take up of software subscriptions has been slower than expected	Included in above	product sales data	Daniel P.	19 July	True/ False	...
Churn is the main reason why software subscription sales is slow	Chart showing customer retention rate (y-axis) over the last 3 years (x-axis)	customer sales data	Sarah K.	17 July	True/ False	...
Average invoice price is declining with growth in discounts and promotions	Chart showing average deal pricing and discount (y-axis) over the last 3 years (x-axis)	customer sales data	Sarah K.	19 July	True/ False	...
Fixed costs remains flat YoY despite loss of revenue which is further compressing margins	Chart showing fixed costs and operating profits and margins (y-axis) over the last 3 years (x-axis)	P&L: fixed costs, profits and margins	Sarah K.	21 July	True/ False	...
...	...	...	...	...	...	...

Figure AI.3: work plan to prove/disprove and quantify issues

- customer data, including
  - customer accounts
  - purchase history
  - annual spend
  - profitability
- employee data, including
  - organisation charts
  - contact information
  - salary and wage costs by employee
- stakeholders and debtors
- competitor information.

3. Analyse data and draw conclusions

Data and analyses are used to prove or disprove each issue, understand the severity of each and provide a basis from which to draw conclusions. If issues are already known to management — such as shortage of cash in distressed situations — the value of the analysis is not in identifying the problem but in revealing how serious it is. The type of analyses used and the presentation of information are tailored to the issues, but some useful approaches are presented in figures AI.4 to AI.7 (overleaf), and include P&L, balance sheet and cash flow trends, financial ratios, cost structure analysis and return on capital employed (ROCE) analysis.

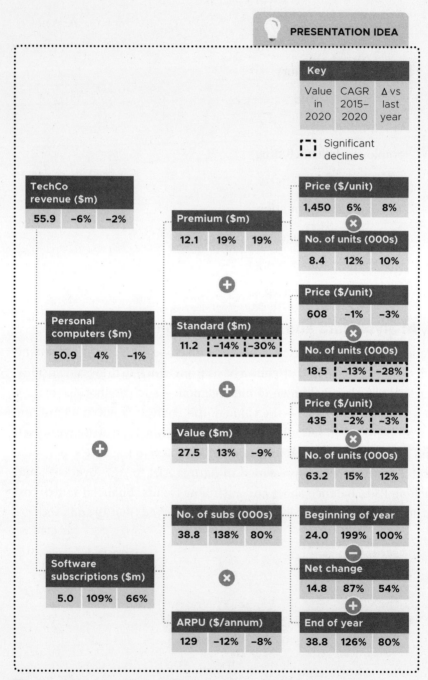

Figure AI.4: identifying financial and operating trends

RATIO	Y–3	Y–2	Y–1	CY	Y+1	Y+2	Y+3
Return on capital employed (ROCE)	[x]	[x]	[x]	[x]	[x]	[x]	[x]
EBITDA	[x]	[x]	[x]	[x]	[x]	[x]	[x]
Capital employed	[x]	[x]	[x]	[x]	[x]	[x]	[x]
Return on invested capital (ROIC)	[x]	[x]	[x]	[x]	[x]	[x]	[x]
NOPLAT = EBITDA after taxes (30%)	[x]	[x]	[x]	[x]	[x]	[x]	[x]
Invested capital = Capital employed	[x]	[x]	[x]	[x]	[x]	[x]	[x]
Return on Equity (ROE)	[x]	[x]	[x]	[x]	[x]	[x]	[x]
Net current profit	[x]	[x]	[x]	[x]	[x]	[x]	[x]
Equity	[x]	[x]	[x]	[x]	[x]	[x]	[x]
Net debt / EBITDA multiple	[x]	[x]	[x]	[x]	[x]	[x]	[x]
Net debt	[x]	[x]	[x]	[x]	[x]	[x]	[x]
EBITDA	[x]	[x]	[x]	[x]	[x]	[x]	[x]
Liquidity ratio	[x]	[x]	[x]	[x]	[x]	[x]	[x]
Current assets	[x]	[x]	[x]	[x]	[x]	[x]	[x]
Current liabilities	[x]	[x]	[x]	[x]	[x]	[x]	[x]
Acid test	[x]	[x]	[x]	[x]	[x]	[x]	[x]
Current assets excl. inventories	[x]	[x]	[x]	[x]	[x]	[x]	[x]
Current liabilities	[x]	[x]	[x]	[x]	[x]	[x]	[x]
Leverage	[x]	[x]	[x]	[x]	[x]	[x]	[x]
Net debt	[x]	[x]	[x]	[x]	[x]	[x]	[x]
Equity	[x]	[x]	[x]	[x]	[x]	[x]	[x]

Figure AI.5: ratio analysis: financial performance and risk

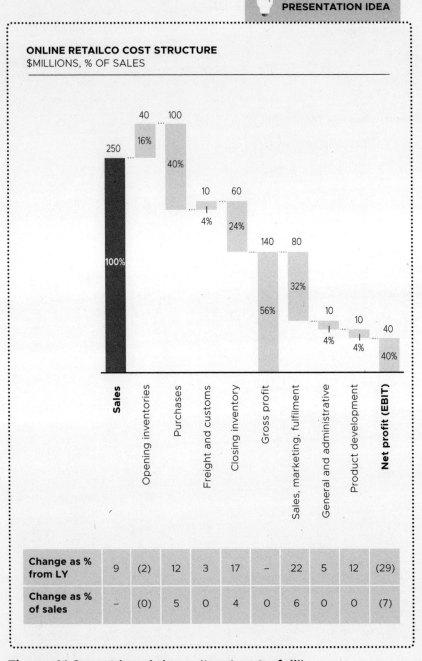

Figure AI.6: cost breakdown ('cost waterfall')

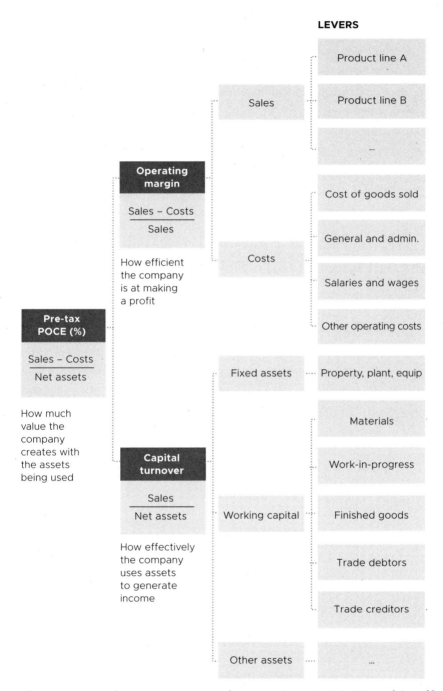

LEVERS

Figure AI.7: using return on capital employed (ROCE) to identify improvements

4. Refine issues

An 'ingoing hypothesis' on the issues facing the company enables the diagnosis to home in on key areas of concern; however, the list should be refined continuously over the course of the diagnostic. Based on interviews and analysis of the data, new issues may emerge that will need to be added to the initial list. At the same time, previously assumed issues may prove insignificant once the data is understood, so that further analysis will be unnecessary. This iterative approach, through regular updates to the issues list and ongoing prioritisation, ensures that the diagnostic is comprehensive while remaining focused on the topics of key importance (think 80/20 rule).

5. Present findings and actions

The final step is to present the diagnostic results and establish executive alignment on the response plan, including: (1) identify issues and type of response required; (2) identify and recommend any short-term actions — for example, capture quick wins or address urgent operational or financial issues; and (3) recommend the implementation approach and agree on next steps to develop a strategic response that fully addresses challenges and opportunities.

APPENDIX II: MONITORING AND IMPROVING CASH FLOWS

Cash flow is the lifeblood of a company. If a company faces a cash squeeze, managing cash flows and liquidity by establishing effective systems and processes becomes vitally important, as 'early warning systems' enable the proactive identification of interventions that can prevent shortages of cash or insolvent trading. At a minimum, the company must remain a going concern by being able to pay its debts as and when they fall due *and* continue to remain solvent for at least 12 months from the end of the reporting period.

Actively managing cash over short time horizons, especially when cash needs are a priority, can benefit from centralising cash management in a Cash War Room or Cash Lab to understand the existing cash position and to create ongoing visibility and transparency. The Cash Lab concept (see figure AII.1, overleaf) provides a comprehensive approach to cash management that involves monitoring and forecasting the company's cash flow position, identifying and prioritising options to manage anticipated shortfalls or gaps, and executing cash generation and savings initiatives to achieve set cash targets. Typically, the Cash Lab is operated by the Finance department but is embedded in the operations of the transformation office or similar centralised PMO, which provides the linkages and coordination to capture regular input from each department, sustain regular cash review meetings, and maintain oversight of cash management initiatives to ensure progress.

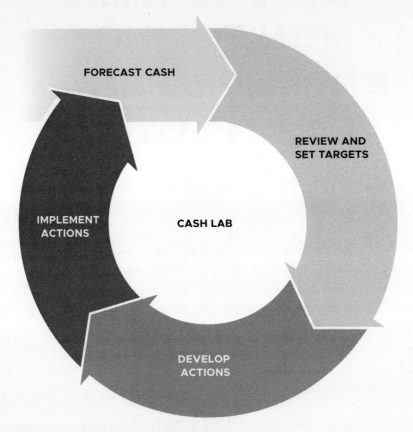

Figure AII.1: the cash lab concept

The key activities involved in establishing and operating a Cash Lab can be managed across four steps:

1. Build cash forecast model

Establishing a reliable cash forecast model is at the heart of providing transparency and visibility in relation to the company's cash flow. The starting point is to build a cash prediction model based on current and historical cash flow figures, and to verify that the process of recording cash flow and the figures themselves are reliable.[11] These figures then form key input into the financial model. Each cash inflow and outflow is projected into the future, taking into account any key assumptions and the cash impact of any planned initiatives. Once established, the financial model can then be used for planning purposes, as well as the basis for daily, monthly and quarterly reporting on cash flow projections. The model should be able to answer key questions about the company's cash position, including:

- What is the current cash outlook for the company — short-term, mid-term and long-term?

- What are the major cash inflows and outflows and how are they expected to change over time?

- What cash reserves are required to cover the company's current and future cash requirements?

2. Review cash position and targets

Preparation for cash review meetings typically requires each division to complete a template with their most up-to-date cash flow forecast. These are collated by the TO and used as input in the cash prediction model to produce updated reports. Reviews of the company's cash position should be held regularly (at least monthly) to discuss liquidity requirements of the company and to control and monitor the use of cash by each division. Typical agenda items for discussion are:

- overall summary of current cash flow position

- review of variance between budgeted and actual cash level, and variance from the prior month

- review of individual transactions for evaluation, comment and approval.

The overall cash position should be managed to *clearly defined targets* determined by the overall cash requirements of the company. The minimum level of cash the company should generate from operations, sometimes measured as Free Funds from Operations (FFO), needs to be sufficient to service debts — that is, it should not fall below the level of debt repayments and interest due. Additionally, targets should factor in a liquidity buffer, and start to capture any emerging cash needs to support the overall transformation program — for example, cash to selectively build new capabilities or support capital build programs.

3. Determine cash initiatives

If cash shortages are anticipated (a variance between actual cash flow and cash flow targets), actions will be required to close the gap. Pinpointing the most effective actions to take requires that cash levers be identified and prioritised to determine the sources of greatest leverage. Operating expenses, capital structure and capital turnover all provide a range of levers for improving a company's cash position. Prioritisation and selection of initiatives should consider the feasibility and impact of each lever to develop a ranked list of initiatives. The size of the gap and the urgency to close it will determine the scope of cash management efforts. Initiatives frequently used to drive near-term cash improvements are outlined in figure 1.1 (pp. 6–7), and typically include:

- *Overhead reductions.* Manage expense practices ranging from mild to harsh.

- *Fixed cost reductions.* Establish a fixed cost reduction plan and mobilise a dedicated team, typically with multiple waves of refinement.

- *Borrowing program.* Raise additional funding to cover liabilities — by means of a rescue package from creditors, for example.

- *capex review.* Triage, reprioritise and re-budget capital investments that are planned and underway to optimise their timing and impact.

- *Asset sale.* Prepare asset sale plans and dispose of non-core assets to unlock cash on the balance sheet.

4. Implement cash initiatives

Implementation should involve executing and managing cash initiatives as a program. This involves the ongoing coordination, tracking and review of activities. In financially distressed companies it is not unusual to put in place a portfolio of cash initiatives that simultaneously operate on multiple levers to form a substantive response plan that addresses urgent cash shortages. Short-term cash management actions are then typically integrated into forecasts. Execution of cash initiatives may be supported through the TO, which assists in developing implementation plans and the tracking and coordinating initiatives between Finance and divisions.

APPENDIX III: DEFINING ASPIRATIONS IN A WORKSHOP

An effective, low-risk approach to defining company aspirations and strategy, and building consensus among the management team, is an interactive, structured one- to two-day offsite workshop and/or series of workshops for top management. The use of an offsite facilitates the collaborative definition of the company's aspirations and encourages the development of the content and key decisions that shape the strategic blueprint. At the same time, participant involvement fosters commitment and is an opportunity to see how the management team work together.

Key to a successful management offsite is to establish upfront a clear workshop purpose, a carefully designed approach to achieve that purpose, and sufficient preparation beforehand with strong facilitation on the day. Good facilitation assists good decision making and leads the team towards consensus with an energised management team. Ideally, facilitators who coordinate and manage activities on the day are independent, with no vested interests. Once the offsite has been held it's important to follow up with participants and ensure closure of any decisions or actions.

Drawing on the earlier material developed in the case for change (chapter 2), preparation for the management offsite should make use of the fact base to highlight how the company has recently performed and future industry and market trends, and it should draw out the implications for the future of the company. Additionally, strategic choices and solution options should be developed in advance of the workshop, taking into consideration relevant aspects of the fact base, including: the customer value chain in which the company participates; the company's assets and capabilities; and case studies from competitors and other companies.

An overall suggested approach for using workshops to define aspirations, prioritise areas for the company to focus on and develop strategic options follows four steps:

1. Establish the workshop purpose

Clearly identify what needs to be achieved:

- Define aspiration and targets for the company.
- Determine which areas of the company to focus on (markets, BUs or functions).
- Agree and prioritise pain points and issues that need to be addressed.
- Generate solution options, including both quick wins and longer term initiatives.

2. Design the approach

Select and design a workshop that best suits the audience in order to achieve its purpose. It could include some or all of the following approaches:

- *speaker presentations* — internal or external speaker shares topics and content with participants to inform, inspire or motivate; could involve the company's customers, industry experts or key executives

- *gallery walks* — a presentation method where participants walk round a gallery of exhibits to reflect on historical performance and identify areas to prioritise and focus on; sometimes called mirror workshops

- *questionnaires/surveys* — the collection of data during the workshop that can be analysed either in real time, to shape workshop proceedings and activities, or afterwards, to inform post-workshop decision making and actions

- *focus groups / breakouts* — discussions, brainstorming and idea generation. Participants develop ideas and contribute content; typically involves breaking into smaller groups to discuss and prepare Post-it notes and flip-charts

- *prioritisation activity* — collaborative exploration and ranking of content against criteria or to determine relative importance; may involve grouping content into themes and applying a method of scoring to reach consensus across a group

- *simulations* — interactive activities that enable participants to explore concepts and experience results first-hand; very useful for frontline transformations involving process or customer content.

3. Plan and deliver the day

The practical organisation and preparation required to set up and operate the workshop includes the following:

- *determine attendees and structure* — decide who will attend (for example, decision makers, key influencers, topic experts)

- *develop agenda* — for each of the workshop components decide the sequence, allotted time, facilitator or presenter (running order)

- *prepare workshop content* — ensure materials are developed and finalised (print handouts, large-format printing, stationery, materials or props)

- *prepare venue, logistics, setup.*

4. Close post-workshop actions

During the workshop agree on the next steps required and post-workshop actions to ensure objectives are met:

- Set and agree on any milestones and timeline for achieving workshop objectives, including final sign-off.

- Complete and distribute workshop content (outputs, decisions, agreed next steps, timelines for final sign-off).

- Action next steps to support the workshop objectives (offline work to investigate, trial an idea, solve a problem, provide input or validation).

ENDNOTES

Chapter 1

1 See for example SAFe® 4.6 Introduction: Overview of the Scaled Agile Framework® for Lean Enterprises.

2 Responsible for ensuring product outcomes are delivered and represents the voice of the customer.

3 Facilitates the delivery process, removes barriers and promotes cooperation across roles and functions.

4 Individuals who form part of a cross-functional team that is self-organising and empowered.

Chapter 2

5 The link between company performance and market factors dates back to the Structure–Conduct–Performance framework developed in the 1930s (Mason), which later contributed to the development of competitive strategy concepts in the 1980s (Porter).

6 UN E-government survey, 2018.

Chapter 3

7 Leading robotic process automation vendors include Blue Prism, UiPath and Automation Anywhere; other common tools include chatbots and virtual assistants.

Chapter 4

8 Hughes, M. (2011). 'Do 70 Per Cent of All Organizational Change Initiatives Really Fail?' *Journal of Change Management* 11:4, 451–64.

9 This included direct responsibility for a £2.1 billion annual budget, assets of £17 billion and 30 000 employees.

Chapter 5

10 Common collaboration tools include Slack, Kanban, Group Chat, Google Docs and @mentions.

Appendix II

11 If an existing cash flow model is already in use within the company, the existing model should be reviewed to confirm the methodology is acceptable and that the model can be flexed based on new assumptions and scenarios.

ABOUT THE AUTHORS

Michael Vullings is a business leader and executive with a passion and the expertise to unlock the potential of teams and organisations. He has a record of successfully leading, managing and advising large and complex organisations on transformational change. He has helped top companies respond to digital disruption and  navigate pressing challenges to achieve breakthrough results. Michael started his career in management consulting and then gained deep-sector expertise in the telecommunications, media and technology industry, in which he has built a reputation for delivering quick-win initiatives alongside lasting improvements. His qualifications include B Laws (LLB), B Comm (Media), M ProfAcc, M Arts and M CorpGvnce, obtained from leading universities in Australia.

Graham Christie is an accomplished entrepreneur, marketing executive and commercial leader. He is an expert in customer-led transformation and has advised major corporations on executing change and transformation strategies and achieving breakthrough performance in corporate innovation and entrepreneurship programs. Graham has deep experience in both client-side and market services roles in the telecommunications, media and technology industry. He co-founded and led the international expansion of an award-winning technology and services business. As a pioneer in mobile customer marketing and communications, Graham was the inaugural chairperson of the Mobile Council on the Interactive Advertising Bureau. He is a director, investor and start-up mentor.

INDEX